FLASHBACKS

TWENTY-FIVE YEARS OF DOONESBURY

FLASHBACKS
TWENTY-FIVE YEARS OF DOONESBURY

G.B. Trudeau

Andrews and McMeel
A Universal Press Syndicate Company
Kansas City

DOONESBURY is distributed internationally by Universal Press Syndicate.

Flashbacks: Twenty-Five Years of Doonesbury copyright ©1995 by G.B. Trudeau. All rights reserved. Printed in the United States of America. No part of this book may be used or reproduced in any manner whatsoever without written permission except in the case of reprints in the context of reviews. For information, write Andrews and McMeel, a Universal Press Syndicate Company, 4900 Main Street, Kansas City, Missouri 64112.

Library of Congress Catalog Card Number: 95-77566

ISBN: 0-8362-0436-0 (paperback)
         0-8362-0437-9 (hardback)

Design by Jessica Helfand and Melissa Tardiff, the Jessica Helfand Studio

THIS BOOK IS DEDICATED TO JANE —
WIFE, FRIEND, MOVIE COMPANION,
TAKE-OUT SPECIALIST,
AND ALL-AROUND FABULOUS BABE

A Few Words from the Author

AT SOME unspecified point in mid-life, one suddenly starts paying closer attention to compliments, holding on to them as if each might be the last. "What a nice hat," for instance, becomes as valued as, "Great merger, guy!" In evolutionary terms, this is a significant advance from the sense of fraudulence that attends even the faintest praise for the tiny triumphs of youth. Once well beyond the possibility of wunderkindom, with options closing behind you with the finality of steel doors, it becomes necessary to find in kind words some hint that you've lived your life to good purpose — or failing that, to maximum effect.

Maximum effect has always been my fallback position. I know what a life of good purpose is — there were plenty in my family who embodied it — but I chose, I believe, the tougher route. I say tougher, because anyone can be beloved. Well, not anyone, but if you're willing to set aside fifty years of your life to the service of others, it can be done. Far more difficult is *not* leading the communitarian, civic-minded life, but somehow seeming *of* it. This is the lie that people in daily journalism live. In the case of the political cartoonist, it's a lie that people generally see through.

A favorite cartoon panel of mine, done some years ago by the late B. Kliban, showed a cartoonist walking down the street, resplendent in ascot and smoking jacket, undraped women draped on either arm, with a policeman clearing the sidewalk of the common rabble before him. As the officer sends a hapless pedestrian sprawling into traffic, he bellows, "Get out of the way, you swine — a cartoonist is coming!"

The joke, of course, depends entirely on the common understanding that society accords the cartoonist no respect whatsoever. Indeed, it is not unusual for a reader to approach me with the following approbation: "I so enjoy your . . . your . . . column." This is invariably followed by an expression of relief that he or she has managed to convey admiration for my work while sparing us both the embarrassment of actually naming it.

Why does the centuries-old art of satiric drawing invite such scorn? Well, partly because it richly deserves it. It comes by its vulgarity quite honestly, requiring a broad, popular audience to survive. Just ask any syndicated European cartoonist, of which there are none. What the beaux-arts world knows but can't admit is that pandering is a lot harder than its working definition seems to imply. If this were not so, everyone would be rich and famous and there'd be no one left to apply for NEA grants.

The other reason that my craft is held in such low regard, I think, has to do with its ephemeral nature. Who reads yesterday's papers? The cartoonist's targets — picked off from the passing parade — are usually quickly forgotten in the larger sweep of history. All the more reason, of course, that villains should be laid low with dispatch; ridicule must be timely if it is to be socially useful. There is a genteel school of satire that holds that the practitioner should spare the individual and attack the larger vice. Such satirists are more correctly called humorists, as they usually have nothing more in mind than to plumb public sentiment for a good laugh. There is a certain kind of joke — the good-natured, Will Rogers-style put-down of politicians for their hypocrisy or lawyers for their greed — that is at heart profoundly cynical, because categorical attacks leave no room for hope.

This explains, I suppose, my personal taste for the ad hominem. I prefer to attack a Dan Rostenkowski or a Johnny Cochran in the specific, because such satire implies — or should — that there are moral choices in life, that not everyone behaves this way, and with reason.

Mort Sahl tells the story of visiting a writer on the set of *Saturday Night Live* during its early, headier days. A skit about Henry Kissinger had been scheduled, so Sahl, who kept voluminous files about the Secretary of State, coyly asked the writer why he was attacking Kissinger. "Because he's in charge," came the self-satisfied reply. That was all. Nothing about Vietnam. Or Chile. Not a word about the criminal bombing of Cambodia. The motivation was nothing more than the banal, adolescent need to strike at someone in authority.

Now this is profitable work if you can get it, and you usually can, since scorched-earth humor took off soon thereafter — spreading its spawn across the breadth of the entertainment industry. But it did seem to Sahl — and to me — a lost opportunity, that it was a pity that so much of this smart, caustic, irony-driven satire didn't aim higher, didn't even try to illuminate. Moreover, the humorist without humility, floating above it all, misses the fattest target of them all — himself. It's a target that the greats — Mark Twain, Woody Allen, Jules Feiffer — never took their eyes off of. When Walt Kelly wrote that we have met the enemy and he may be us, he was telling us that the human comedy is all-inclusive, that we're all in the same leaky boat together.

This is why *Doonesbury* is populated by other characters besides the politicians. I need proxies, loyal representatives of my own sovereign state of confusion. As Steve Martin says, comedy isn't pretty. Twenty five years into it, I'm still trying to get it right. The strip remains a work in progress, an imperfect chronicle of human imperfection.

There are many who cannot escape their share of responsibility in this enterprise, and to all I extend my profound thanks. Among them are my wife, Jane; my inking assistant and friend of 24 years, Don Carlton; my trusty sounding board and book editor, David Stanford; my long-time strip editor and human firewall, Lee Salem; Mike Seeley, who runs the office with gracious efficiency; and, of course, Kathy Andrews and my large family of friends and colleagues at Universal Press Syndicate. If I fail to include my boss, John McMeel, it is only for the best of reasons: We are in the middle of contract negotiations.

Garry Trudeau
October 18, 1995

1970~1974

"Yes, dammit.
I'm the model for Michael."
—GARRY TRUDEAU, 1971

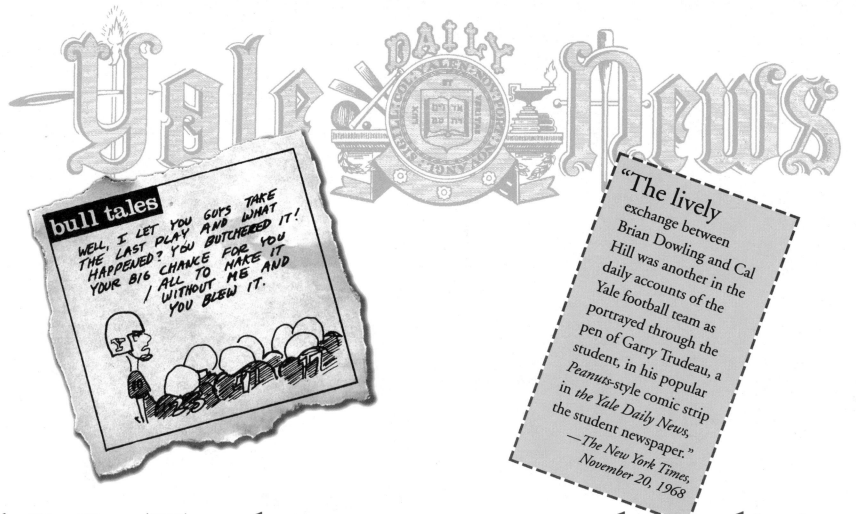

"The lively exchange between Brian Dowling and Cal Hill was another in the daily accounts of the Yale football team as portrayed through the pen of Garry Trudeau, a student, in his popular *Peanuts*-style comic strip in *the Yale Daily News*, the student newspaper."

—The New York Times, November 20, 1968

"G.B. Trudeau never made a diving catch in the end zone with 30 seconds to go, but he thought about it a lot."

—NEW HAVEN REGISTER, MARCH 1, 1970

September 30 **1968**

Bull Tales, by G.B. Trudeau, first appears in *Yale Daily News* and within a few weeks attracts the attention of Universal Press Syndicate co-founder and editor, James F. Andrews.

Trudeau's other passion: third-string intramural hockey.

HAPPY
HALLOWEEN
YOURSELF!

October 26 **1970**

Renamed after its principal character, *Doonesbury* debuts in 28 newspapers.

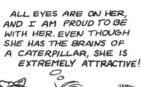

Q ···· Fluke start, right?

A ···· Pretty much. I was approached about syndication during my junior year in college, after an arduous four-week apprenticeship on the school paper. Incredibly, the offer didn't strike me as particularly remarkable. It was the very essence of being in the right place at the right time, but when you're young, you don't understand serendipity. You feel entitled, even to your accidents.

Trudeau makes the first of the only two television appearances of his career, on "To Tell the Truth." Three of the four panelists fail to correctly guess his identity; Trudeau wins $167 and a pair of cuff links.

Comic strip fame brought costume jewelry.

July 17 **1971**

Doonesbury escapes cancellation in a *Macon Telegraph* readers' referendum. For *Doonesbury*, 27; against, 22. It is the first of many such polls taken around the country.

Q— I really wish you would print a picture of Garry Trudeau who draws the fantastic *Doonesbury* cartoon. Those people are super cool.—*L.E., Saugus*
A—Here's super cool Trudeau.

—*The Boston Globe, 1972*

The post-surgeon-general Belmondo pose was soon withdrawn.

—ART BUCHWALD

A legacy terrorist: Phred's father had
harassed the French

27

THANKS FOR COVERING THE CEREMONY, NICHOLE. YOU HELPED ME OUT OF A REAL JAM

GLAD TO DO IT, MIKE

STICK AROUND FOR A SECOND WHILE I PROOFREAD YOUR ARTICLE, O.K.?

O.K...I THINK YOU'LL LIKE IT. EVEN THOUGH I'M JUST A WOMAN, I WROTE IT WITH THE SAME SENSITIVITY ONE FINDS IN YOUR OWN PROSE!

...HMM.. WE'LL SEE... "TODAY PRESIDENT KING AND SPECIAL ASSISTANT CHUCK TAYLOR PRESIDED OVER THE PRESENTATION OF THE NEW UNIVERSITY ART GALLERY."

"MR. KING, THE PERT FATHER OF THREE, LOOKED STUNNING IN HIS PROVOCATIVE MOHAIR SUIT AS HE FLASHED A SMILE AT NEARBY ADMIRERS."

"MR. TAYLOR, THE HUSBAND OF MRS. CHARLES TAYLOR, AND STILL A SVELTE, FIRM 30-32-30, TURNED MORE THAN ONE HEAD WITH HIS SHEER, SKIN-TIGHT SOCKS. CHUCK, A SPECIAL ASSISTANT, IS A FORMER BRUNETTE."

YOU'RE TRYING TO MAKE A POINT HERE, AREN'T YOU?

Q ···· You got caught up in feminism pretty early, didn't you?

A ···· Yes, in early 1970, only seven months after Gloria Steinem reportedly signed on. Seven months is 14 years in pig time. I found that out when I moved to a ski resort, where the locals were a full generation away from getting it. Whenever I brought up the subject, people would dive through the windows. Even the women shunned me, which was pitiful, because the whole point, of course, was to get dates.

First stop, Cleveland.

A Sunday strip about Zonker, kids, and hashish brings down a firestorm of criticism. One Texas editor is awakened by an irate minister on his doorstep early in the morning.

"I also had threats from Abilene and Paris, Texas.... Paris even ran a letter of apology to their readers and said they would refuse to deliver the entire section if it happened again. I think the thing that disturbed most of the publishers is that professional school administrators were the leaders of the protests."
—*Charles O. Kilpatrick, Editor,* San Antonio News, *in a letter to UPS president John McMeel*

Q ···· The hashish strip. What was the deal there?

A ···· I'm not sure. I was 24. It was 1972. Someone once asked Robert Crumb why he drew his infamous incest cartoon. He replied, "I think I was just being a punk." There may have been some of that.

May 10 **1973**

The unanticipated resignation of Watergate conspirator John Ehrlichman causes the recall of a week of strips.

NICHOLE, HAVE YOU HEARD ABOUT MARK'S NEW SERIES OF PROFILES ON HIS RADIO SHOW?

NO. WHAT'S IT ON?

THE WATERGATE CONSPIRATORS. HE'S WORKED OUT COMPLETE BIOGRAPHIES ON ALL OF THEM.

BOY, I'LL BET THEY'RE JUST **BRUTAL!**

NOT AT ALL. I READ THEM LAST NIGHT. SOME OF THEM ARE QUITE SENSITIVE.

"LOS ANGELES IS A LONELY TOWN TO GROW UP IN, ESPECIALLY IF YOU'RE A SMALL BOY NAMED H.R. HALDEMAN."

GOOD NEWS, KIDDIES! TIME FOR ANOTHER EXCLUSIVE WBBY "**WATERGATE PROFILE**"! TODAY'S OBITUARY— **JOHN MITCHELL!**

JOHN MITCHELL, THE FORMER U.S. ATTORNEY-GENERAL, HAS IN RECENT WEEKS BEEN REPEATEDLY LINKED WITH BOTH THE WATERGATE CAPER AND ITS COVER-UP.

IT WOULD BE A DISSERVICE TO MR. MITCHELL AND HIS CHARACTER TO PREJUDGE THE MAN, BUT EVERYTHING KNOWN TO DATE COULD LEAD ONE TO CONCLUDE HE'S GUILTY!

THAT'S **GUILTY!** GUILTY, GUILTY, GUILTY!!

HOLY MOLY, CAMPERS! TIME FOR ANOTHER **WBBY** "**WATERGATE PROFILE**"! TODAY'S COVER-UP CUTIE IS... **JOHN EHRLICHMAN!**

"JOHN EHRLICHMAN, THE PRESIDENT'S ADVISOR ON DOMESTIC AFFAIRS, HAS FOR FOUR YEARS BEEN A CONSIDERABLE POWER IN THE WHITE HOUSE. YET UNTIL RECENTLY, MANY AMERICANS WERE UNAWARE OF THE SCOPE OF HIS DUTIES!"

"ON THE AVERAGE DAY JOHN EHRLICHMAN USED TO CONSULT WITH MR. NIXON AT LEAST ONCE OR TWICE. IF THE WORD CAME DOWN HE WAS NEEDED, HE'D MAKE HIS WAY UP TO THE OVAL OFFICE WHERE HE WOULD INVARIABLY ENCOUNTER FELLOW STAFFER H.R. HALDEMAN!"

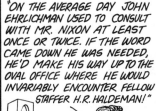

HALT! STOP OR I'LL SHOOT!

BOB! IT'S ME! IT'S ME!

> **"** I hear my resignation fouled up your series. Sorry. Next time, let me know what you are planning, and I'll try to cooperate. **"**

—JOHN EHRLICHMAN
in a letter to Trudeau

The Washington Post tells its readers, "If anyone is going to find any defendant guilty, it's going to be the due process of justice, not a comic strip artist." The editor of The Boston Globe gives a $50 bonus to the copy editor who flagged the offending strip, explaining, "There are bold graphics involved."

June 4 1973

Stars and Stripes announces that *Doonesbury* has become "too political" and drops it. When the paper receives nearly 300 letters of protest, mainly from young enlisted men and their families, the strip is reinstated.

40

GOOD EVENING. PRESIDENT NIXON AND SOVIET CHIEF BREZHNEV ENGAGED IN ANOTHER ROUND OF VIGOROUS TALKS TODAY.

IT WAS LATER ANNOUNCED THAT THEY HAD REACHED AGREEMENT ON A NEW BILATERAL PENAL REFORM PROGRAM, WITH A MUTUAL EXCHANGE OF PRISONERS.

UNDER THE NEW ACCORD, THE U.S. WILL SEND THE SOVIETS THREE BLACK MILITANTS, FOUR RADICAL PRIESTS, AND FIFTY ASSORTED DRAFT DODGERS.

IN RETURN, THE U.S. WILL RECEIVE FIVE POETS, TWO BALLET DANCERS, AND A NOBEL PRIZE LAUREATE.

MARK! WHAT'RE **YOU** DOING HOME?

HI, DAD! I JUST CAME HOME TO HELP YOU RAKE THE BACK YARD!

I BEG YOUR PARDON? YOU CAME HOME TO **HELP**?

SURE. IT'S A PRETTY BIG JOB, AND I THOUGHT..

YOU WERE EXPELLED.. IS THAT IT? OR JUST SUSPENDED?

HUH?.. OF **COURSE NOT!** I JUST CAME HOME TO HELP RAKE THE...

IT'S A GIRL, THEN, RIGHT? SOME POOR GIRL...

LEAVES, DAD! TO RAKE THE **LEAVES!**

MARK, SON, HAVE YOU GIVEN ANY THOUGHT TO THE SORT OF JOB YOU WANT WHEN YOU GRADUATE?

OH, SURE..

I DON'T KNOW WHAT **FIELD** IT'LL BE IN, BUT I KNOW THAT IT WILL HAVE TO BE CREATIVE – A POSITION OF RESPONSIBILITY, BUT NOT ONE THAT RESTRICTS PERSONAL FREEDOM..

IT MUST PAY FAIRLY WELL;.. THE ATMOSPHERE, RELAXED, INFORMAL; MY COLLEAGUES, INTERESTING, MELLOW, AND NOT TOO CONCERNED WITH A STRUCTURED WORKING SITUATION.

IN SHORT, YOU HAVE NO INTENTION OF GETTING A JOB.

I DIDN'T **SAY** THAT.

STATE YOUR NAME AND OCCUPATION, PLEASE.

MY NAME IS **PHRED**. I'M AN INSURGENT FOR THE PATHET LAO, CURRENTLY ON FURLOUGH. I'M A NATIVE OF HUÉ, VIETNAM.

AND THE GENTLEMAN NEXT TO YOU?

I'M HIS DISTINGUISHED COUNSEL.

The *Lincoln Journal* becomes the first paper to move *Doonesbury* from the comic page to the editorial page. In the years that follow, many other papers follow suit.

I AM AN OLD WOMAN, SIRS. I KNOW NOTHING OF POLITICS. I KNOW ONLY THAT THE AIRPLANE CAME AND DESTROYED MY VILLAGE.

BUT CAN YOU BE SURE IT WAS AN **AMERICAN** PLANE, MS. LOO? THIS, OF COURSE, IS OF VITAL IMPORTANCE!

YOU SEE, MS. LOO, THERE ARE MANY DIFFERENT KINDS OF PLANES — THERE ARE BIG ONES, LITTLE ONES, JET PLANES AND..

IT WAS A NAVY McDONNELL F4B-1 PHANTOM II.

OH, YES, THAT'S OURS.

MR. PHRED, THE COMMITTEE WOULD LIKE TO THANK YOU FOR ORGANIZING SO EFFECTIVELY ALL THE TESTIMONY WE HAVE HEARD TO DATE.

NOW THEN, HAVE YOU ITEMIZED THOSE MEASURES YOU DEEM NECESSARY FOR A SHORT-TERM CESSATION OF THE SUFFERING OF SOUTHEAST ASIAN REFUGEES?

YES, SENATOR. COUNSEL AND I HAVE PREPARED A LIST OF WHAT WE FEEL ARE THE **MINIMAL** MATERIALS REQUIRED TO ALLEVIATE THE CURRENT CRISIS.. PROCEED.

3.5 MILLION SLEEPING BAGS...

HOLD IT.

GOODNESS KNOWS I TRIED TO TELL HER, JEAN! "MOMMY," I SAID, "WHAT'S WITH ALL THE BABIES? YOU WANT TO BE A HOUSE-WIFE ALL YOUR LIFE?"

BUT SHE KEEPS TURNIN' 'EM OUT! EVERY YEAR, JUST LIKE CLOCKWORK! IT'S REALLY **AMAZING!**

I DUNNO.. MAYBE I'LL JUST HAVE TO WORK ON MY FATHER INSTEAD..

AS I UNDERSTAND IT, HE FIGURES HEAVILY IN ALL THIS..

OH, YEAH?

MOMMY GOES INTO THE HOSPITAL TODAY. I GUESS I BETTER START THINKING POSITIVELY ABOUT MY NEWEST SIBLING..

GOOD IDEA, DEAR!

I JUST HOPE IT'S A SISTER. I **NEED** A SISTER!

ALSO, IT'S MORE "IN" TO BE A FEMALE THAN A MALE THESE DAYS! MUCH MORE FASHIONABLE.

IT IS?

SURE!

I DON'T THINK THERE'S ANY QUESTION ABOUT IT...

IT'S TRUE. I READ IT IN "TIME" LAST WEEK.

ELLIE! PHONE FOR YOU, DEAR!

HELLO?.. HI, DADDY!.. SHE **DID?** WHAT IS IT?!

IT'S A **WOMAN!**

"WOMAN"?

IT'S A BABY **WOMAN!**

Often printed as a birth announcement, "Baby Woman" became a baby tee, size XXXS.

NICHOLE, THIS HERE IS ROLAND BURTON HEDLEY, JR.! HE'S WRITING A STUDENT STORY FOR A POPULAR NEWSWEEKLY!

WELCOME TO WALDEN, ROLAND.

THANK YOU, NICHOLE. I LIKE YOUR DIGS. THEY'RE REAL NICE!

THANKS. WE LIKE THEM.

ROLAND'S A TOUGH, CYNICAL REPORTER, SO DON'T TRY TO PUT ANYTHING OVER ON HIM— IT'S SIMPLY USELESS TO PRETEND THERE'S NOT A LOT OF CASUAL SEX AND DRUGS OUT HERE.

THERE IS?!

OH, ME AND MY BIG MOUTH!

YOU KNOW, MY EDITORS ARE GOING TO BE VERY ASTONISHED WHEN THEY HEAR HOW YOU PEOPLE LIVE. WE ALL THOUGHT STUDENTS WERE BACK IN THE LIBRARIES, FILLED WITH GRIM SERIOUSNESS OF PURPOSE!

DON'T GET ME WRONG— I'M NOT SHOCKED OR ANYTHING— I WENT TO HARVARD, AND WE HAD SOME PRETTY ZANY PEOPLE THERE, I CAN TELL YOU!

BUT YOU GUYS ARE CRAZY!— YOU INGEST WEIRD DRUGS! YOU LIVE IN TOTAL DECADENCE! YOU DON'T DO ANY WORK!

LET'S FACE IT— YOU GUYS ARE STILL HIPPIES!

GASP!

WELL, I WANT TO THANK YOU LADS AGAIN. WHAT YOU'VE TOLD ME THIS WEEK IS GOING TO COME AS A REAL SHOCKER TO MY EDITORS!

WELL, THINGS AREN'T ALWAYS WHAT THEY SEEM, ROLAND!

I CAN SEE THAT NOW. AND I CAN'T WAIT TO CORROBORATE THESE FINDINGS!

WHAT? CORROBORATE? ROLAND, YOU DON'T HAVE TO DO THAT! WE'RE VERY TYPICAL!

ARE YOU SURE? ARE YOU POSITIVE OTHER COLLEGE STUDENTS ARE INTO THE SAME THINGS?

WE GIVE YOU OUR WORD OF HONOR WE REPRESENT A NATIONAL TREND!

THAT'S GOOD ENOUGH FOR ME!

SNAP!

CLACKITY!
CLAK! CLACKITY! CLACK

TIME
The New Hedonism

EXTRA! LATEST STUDENT MOOD!

Chicago Trib on sale here

"SEX! SEX AND PEYOTE!" HE REPLIED.

I'M IN BIG TROUBLE..

MR. PRESIDENT, THE APPRAISER, MR. NEWMAN, IS HERE.

SEND HIM IN, AL.

GOOD MORNING, SIR!

GOOD MORNING, RALPH. I HAVE ANOTHER NATIONAL SECURITY MISSION FOR YOU. I WANT YOU TO APPRAISE MY TAPES.

HMM... THIS IS A PRETTY IMPRESSIVE COLLECTION... A LOT OF BIG NAMES... "MARCH 10 WITH HALDEMAN....SEPTEMBER 9 WITH DEAN!.. OH, WOW!! JUNE 20 WITH MITCHELL!

BOY, SIR, THAT'S A REAL COLLECTOR'S ITEM!

YES, IT'S PRETTY HARD TO GET...

HAIG, IT'S ABOUT TIME FOR MY WEEKLY T.V. APPEAL TO THE PEOPLE. CALL PROPS AND TELL THEM TO BRING OVER SOME MORE LINCOLN VISUALS — A BUST, ETCHINGS, ANYTHING!

MR. PRESIDENT, WITH ALL DUE RESPECT, SIR, I THINK YOU'VE JUST ABOUT GONE THE LIMIT ON COMPARISONS OF YOURSELF WITH LINCOLN..

YOU THINK SO?.. HMM. MAYBE YOU'RE RIGHT, AL...

IT WOULD BE THE FIFTH TIME, SIR..

IT'S JUST THAT I CAN'T GET OVER ALL THE PARALLELS!

IT IS EERIE, SIR..

RRRRR..

The prize: 50% off
on large fries.

April 20 **1974**

Joanie Caucus is accepted into law school at Boston University after 300 students sign a petition requesting that she be admitted. Joanie also receives acceptances from Georgetown, Golden Gate State, and U.C. Berkeley. She goes to Berkeley.

*Among Joanie's new classmates:
Zoë Baird*

OF COURSE, DIFFERENT PEOPLE WILL NO DOUBT HAVE VERY DIFFERENT INTERPRETATIONS OF WHAT WAS SAID — PARTICULARLY AT THE SO-CALLED HUSH MONEY MEETING.

IN THIS MEETING, WE DISCUSSED THE OPTIONS WITH GREAT CANDOR. FIRST, WE COULD HAVE PAID THE MONEY, IN THE INTERESTS OF NATIONAL SECURITY. BUT WE MIGHT HAVE BEEN BLED DRY.

OR, WE COULD HAVE TAKEN EVERYONE WITH KNOWLEDGE OF THE CASE OUT AND SHOT THEM. BUT, AS A LAWYER, I KNEW THAT WOULD BE WRONG.

NO, I WANTED TO GET THE WHOLE THING OUT IN THE OPEN!..

P: Another subpoena?! What do those 38 (explitive deleted) maniacs want now?!

St.C: That (characterization omitted) Rodino wants 1250 more tapes!
P: What?!

H: (rushing in) Excuse me, Mr. President, but there's a damn (explitive included) U-Haul pulling up outside!

P: (Unbelievably gross and offensive explitive deleted) Really?

RON, DO YOU THINK THE PRESIDENT'S RECENT MID-EAST TRIP HAS BROUGHT ABOUT ANY INCREASE IN SUPPORT FOR HIM?

ABSOLUTELY! IN FACT, THERE IS NO LONGER ANY DOUBT OF IT...

IN A MAJOR POLL TAKEN LAST WEEK, A WHOPPING 96% OF THE EGYPTIAN PEOPLE THINK THAT THE PRESIDENT IS DOING A GOOD JOB AND SHOULD NOT RESIGN UNTIL HE HAS FINISHED THE WORK HE WAS ELECTED TO DO!!

WE FIND THAT SIGNIFICANT.
YOU WOULD, RON.

Sign Petition Here!
IMPEACH PRESIDENCY NIXON!

..IN SUM, THEN, THE INFORMATION AVAILABLE TO ME AT THIS TIME DOES CORRESPOND TO MY KNOWLEDGE AT THE TIME OF MY PREVIOUS STATEMENT.

THAT WAS BEAUTIFUL, RON.

ANY OTHER QUESTIONS?

YES, I HAVE ONE, RON.

YES, MR. SIDEY?

RON, SOMETIMES I IMAGINE YOU MUST GET UP IN THE MORNING, LOOK IN THE MIRROR BEFORE YOU'VE SHAVEN, AND THINK TO YOURSELF, "RON, YOU'RE ABOUT TO BEGIN ANOTHER DAY OF EVASION AND DECEIT."

HERE'S MY QUESTION, RON: WHAT DO YOU DO AFTER YOU'VE COME TO SUCH A REALIZATION?

I SHAVE.

The San Francisco Chronicle drops *Doonesbury* for one day, resulting in 2,000 calls from irate readers. Berkeley law students hold a press conference to announce their intention to picket, and to sue if the strip is dropped permanently.

MAY 17TH!

Boston on the march--and nobody got hit.

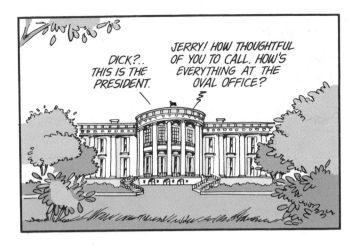

DICK?.. THIS IS THE PRESIDENT.

JERRY! HOW THOUGHTFUL OF YOU TO CALL. HOW'S EVERYTHING AT THE OVAL OFFICE?

NOT ALL THAT IT COULD BE, DICK..

NO? WHAT'S WRONG?

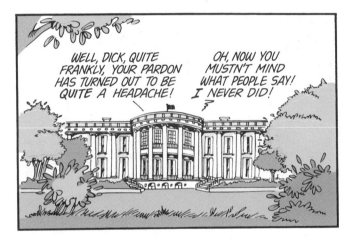

WELL, DICK, QUITE FRANKLY, YOUR PARDON HAS TURNED OUT TO BE QUITE A HEADACHE!

OH, NOW YOU MUSTN'T MIND WHAT PEOPLE SAY! I NEVER DID!

WELL, I PROBABLY WOULDN'T DICK, IF YOU HAD GONE THE CONTRITION ROUTE. BUT YOU DIDN'T — EVEN AFTER MASSIVE INCRIMINATING EVIDENCE!

WELL, THAT'S THE WAY IT HAS TO BE ...

MR. PRESIDENT, MR. PRESIDENT!

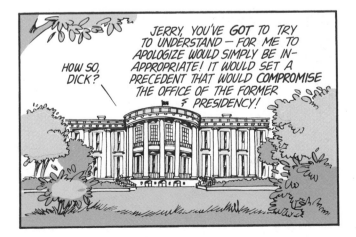

HOW SO, DICK?

JERRY, YOU'VE GOT TO TRY TO UNDERSTAND — FOR ME TO APOLOGIZE WOULD SIMPLY BE IN-APPROPRIATE! IT WOULD SET A PRECEDENT THAT WOULD COMPROMISE THE OFFICE OF THE FORMER PRESIDENCY!

HUH?

YOU SEE, IT'S NOT ME I'M THINKING OF, JER — IT'S FUTURE FORMER PRESIDENTS!

GBTrudeau

61

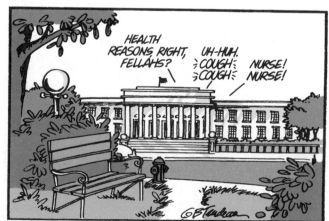

1975~1979

"There is no way to defend his art as Art."
— MERYLE SECREST, ART CRITIC FOR *THE WASHINGTON POST*

Perks: The job came with mansion, limo, drivers, bodyguards, and housegirls.

<blockquote>
"It was a hot, nearly blazing day in Washington, and I was coming down the steps of the Supreme Court when all of a sudden I saw a crowd of people and I heard them saying, 'Uncle Duke.' I looked around, and I recognized people who were total strangers pointing at me and laughing. It was a weird experience, and as it happened I was sort of by myself up there on the stairs, and I thought: What in the fuck madness is going on? Why am I being mocked by a gang of strangers and friends on the steps of the Supreme Court?"
</blockquote>

—HUNTER S. THOMPSON
Writer

May 5 1975

Trudeau becomes the first comic strip artist to win the Pulitzer Prize for Editorial Cartooning. The Editorial Cartoonists' Society passes a resolution condemning the Pulitzer Prize committee. Trudeau, assured the award was irrevocable, supports the resolution.

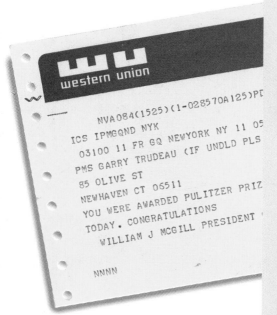

western union

NVA084(1525)(1-028570A125)P
ICS IPMGQND NYK
03100 11 FR GQ NEWYORK NY 11 05
PMS GARRY TRUDEAU (IF UNDLD PLS
85 OLIVE ST
NEWHAVEN CT 06511
YOU WERE AWARDED PULITZER PRIZ
TODAY. CONGRATULATIONS
WILLIAM J MCGILL PRESIDENT

NNNN

> **"** *I'm perfectly thrilled and delighted. I've kept my fingers crossed for fear he might end up in jail.* **"**

—HELEN G. TRUDEAU
to hometown newspaper, upon hearing of her grandson's Pulitzer

Q ···· Why is satire such an effective form of social control?

A ···· Because at its rotten little core, it's unfair. It's rude and uncivil. It lacks balance and proportion, and it obeys none of the normal rules of engagement. Satire picks a one-sided fight, and the more its intended target reacts, the more its practitioner gains the advantage. And as if that weren't enough, this savage, unregulated sport is protected by the United States Constitution. Cool, huh?

An exhibition of Trudeau cartoons opens in Washington, D.C., for the benefit of the National Women's Political Caucus. Reports *The Washington Post*, "Almost 1,000 people tried to get into the small gallery. Observed one disgruntled man, "If these women can't run an art show, how do they expect to run the country?" Sniffs the *Post's* critic, "There is no way to defend his art as Art."

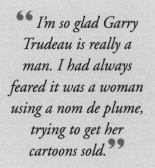

February 10 **1976**

Andy Lippincott, a gay, is introduced in *Doonesbury*, causing dozens of newspapers to drop the sequence. Some papers offer to mail copies of the offending strips to readers.

"We just decided we weren't ready for homosexuality in a comic strip."

—*Miami Herald executive editor Larry Jinks, February 1976*

CHINA, MAC! HENRY'S ASKING ME TO GO TO CHINA!

REALLY?! WHAT A **WON-DERFUL** OPPORTUNITY FOR YOU, SIR!

BUSH HAS BEEN RECALLED, AND THE PRESIDENT WANTS ME TO TAKE OVER AS **TOP ENVOY!**

CHINA'S GOOD FORTUNE IS SAMOA'S MISFORTUNE, SIR. YOU WILL BE SORELY MISSED BY ALL OF US!

I'VE BEEN DIRECTED TO APPEAR AT A SENATE CONFIRMATION HEARING NEXT MONTH..

YOURS HAS BEEN A CAREER OF PUBLIC SERVICE WHICH SAMOANS WILL NOT SOON FORGET!

DO YOU THINK I SHOULD ACCEPT, MAC?

LET US NOT SAY ALOHA, SIR — BUT RATHER, AU REVOIR!

MAC, I THINK I'VE FIGURED OUT WHY THE PRESIDENT'S SENDING ME TO CHINA...

FORD'S TOUGHENING UP, SEE, PLAYING TO THE CONSERVATIVES! TO SHOW THAT HE'S NOT BEING DUPED BY THE REDS, HE'S SENDING A NO-NONSENSE CAREER DIPLOMAT TO PEKING TO INSURE THAT DETENTE IS A TWO-WAY STREET!

SOUNDS REASONABLE. BUT WHY YOU?

MY RECORD HERE, MAC — I'VE SHOWN I KNOW HOW TO WORK WITH MINORITIES!

"MINORITIES"?

AND THAT'S IMPORTANT, MAC — THOSE CHINESE ARE AN ESPECIALLY TRICKY PEOPLE!

THE IMPORTANT THING TO REMEMBER ABOUT THE CHINESE, MAC, IS THAT THEIR PRIMARY CONCERN IS USSR HEGEMONY.

THE CHINESE BELIEVE IN THE INEVITABILITY OF WAR WITH THE RUSKIES. BUT THEY ALSO HAVE AN ABIDING CONVICTION THAT THEY WILL PREVAIL!

THEIR POSITION IS SUMMED UP IN A POPULAR MAOIST SAYING: "THERE IS GREAT DISORDER UNDER HEAVEN AND THE SITUATION IS EXCELLENT."

SOUNDS LIKE ONE OF YOUR PARTIES, SIR.

YEAH, THAT'S WHY I THINK WE'RE GOING TO HIT IT OFF.

December 1 **1975**

Trudeau travels with the press corps covering Gerald Ford's visit to China, and becomes the first American cartoonist to toss a Frisbee on the Great Wall.

The Ugly American Frisbee All-Stars also included the President's daughter, Susan.

Millions of Mao buttons, inescapable in 1975, were to become overnight collector's items.

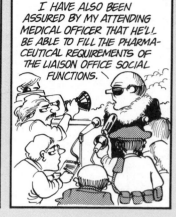

(AND HE BRINGS THE BEST WISHES OF THE AMERICAN PEOPLE.)

YOU KNOW, WHEN I FIRST ARRIVED HERE, I WAS GIVEN MAO'S LITTLE RED BOOK..

(I THINK HE'S ABOUT TO MAKE A JOKE..)

WHEN I ASKED WHY IT WAS SO POPULAR, I WAS TOLD, "BETTER READ THAN DEAD!"

(THE JOKE HAS BEEN MADE, AND HE WILL BE EXPECTING YOU TO LAUGH AT IT. GO WILD.)

HA, **HA** HA, HA! HA! **HEE HEE!** HO, HO! HA!

BUT SERIOUSLY, FOLKS, I'M TICKLED PINKO TO BE HERE TONIGHT...

YOU KNOW, MR. LI, MR. TENG'S SPEECH LEFT ME BAFFLED. WHAT EXACTLY WAS HE GETTING AT?

"THERE IS GREAT DISORDER UNDER HEAVEN, AND THE SITUATION IS EXCELLENT."

I SEE.. WELL, I'D HEARD THAT...

ARE YOU ENJOYING YOUR DINNER?

HUH?..OH, YEAH, ABSOLUTELY! ESPECIALLY THE VEGETABLES— I LOVE YOUR VEGETABLES.

AH, YES—THE VEGETABLES.

SPEAKING OF WHICH, HOW'S THE CHAIRMAN DOING?

"THERE IS CHAOS ON EARTH, AND HIS PULSE IS NORMAL."

TELL ME, MR. LI, HOW DOES THE FOREIGN MINISTRY VIEW NORMALIZATION NOW?

THE CHAIRMAN HAS A SAYING PERTINENT TO YOUR QUESTION.

WELL, I THOUGHT HE MIGHT..

IT IS THIS: "IN A SUITABLE TEMPERATURE, AN EGG BECOMES A CHICKEN, AND THERE ARE NO CHICKENS BORN OF STONES."

FASCINATING.. REALLY VERY FASCINATING..

YOU REALIZE, OF COURSE, THAT IT MAKES NO SENSE WHATSOEVER.

WELL, YOU KNOW, I'VE WONDERED ABOUT THAT..

"I had dinner with the woman who was the basis for the character 'Honey' in *Doonesbury*. I can't say that Tang (Wensheng) seemed particularly thrilled when I blurted out, 'You're Honey' and told her her character was a celebrity in the U.S. She replied, 'Some people have told me it's supposed to be me. But I've never seen the cartoon.' I told her I would mail her some copies of the comic strip. That didn't seem to interest her either."

—*Erik Lacitis, columnist, The Seattle Daily Times*

His Excellency takes the air with love-slave food-taster Honey Huan.

Raved one critic about Thudpucker's single for the Slade campaign: "Sure, it might appear putrid (the B-side is 'Ginny's Song—Disco Version'), but it is appealing enough."

Seven newspapers drop a strip that has Uncle Duke calling President Ford's son a "pot head."

"'There are moments when the press is unfair to anyone who's a public figure,' Ford said, referring to his portrayal as a 'pot head' yesterday in *Doonesbury.* 'But they must make their own moral judgment on that.'"
—*Washington Star, January 20, 1977*

March 22 **1976**

Trudeau is selected as the tenth most admired world figure by high school seniors in a nationwide poll, placing him below Alexander Solzhenitsyn and Ralph Nader, but just ahead of Ronald Reagan and Pope Paul.

Over 30 newspapers drop the strip showing Joanie and Rick in bed together (at the time, neither was married). The editor of *The Huntington Herald-Dispatch* informs his readers, "When I first saw it, I thought it was two guys in bed." *The Bangor Daily News* blocks out the last frame, replacing it with the weather forecast ("Fair, cold, highs in the 30s"). A group of M.I.T. students pickets *The Boston Globe* with signs reading, "Joanie, we forgive you."

Q .... Your family worried, didn't they?

A .... Pretty much incessantly. The accolades, when they happened, came more as a source of relief than pride. My grandmother in particular thought no good could possibly come of cartooning. Every summer when I was growing up she would plead with my parents to send me to Outward Bound, because she had read in *Life* that the counselors were very good at reaching troubled teens.

Q ···· Did they make you go?

A ···· No. In those days, Outward Bound was stocked with the soft sons of the well-off, who, in the absence of war, couldn't think of any other way to build character in their progeny. So they sent them off for three weeks of kayaking and rappelling and subsisting on roots and earthworms, and let's face it, I would have perished. I think my parents knew that.

WHITE HOUSE SYMBOLS. DELACOURT SPEAKING.

DUANE? THIS IS HAM HERE..

I'VE JUST BEEN IN TO SEE JIMMY! HE'S **VERY** PLEASED WITH YOUR WORK, DUANE! THE CALL-IN SHOW. THE CHAT, THE CARDIGAN, THE LIMO CUTS, FULL FINANCIAL DISCLOSURE, AMY'S "TRUSTEE" GOVERNESS — ALL UNEQUIVOCAL HITS!

FACT IS, DUANE, YOUR WORK HAS BECOME TOO IMPORTANT FOR ONLY A SUBCABINET OPERATION! THE PRESIDENT WANTS TO NOMINATE YOU TO A NEW POST—SECRETARY OF SYMBOLISM! WHAT DO YOU SAY, BUDDY?

OKAY BY ME. I DON'T HAVE TO TAKE A PAY RAISE, DO I?

HECK, NO! IN FACT, I'M SURE YOU'VE GOT A CUT COMING TO YOU!

GOOD EVENING. PRESIDENT CARTER'S NOMINEE FOR SECRETARY OF SYMBOLISM, DUANE DELACOURT, HAS GOTTEN OFF TO A RUNNING START.

SPEAKING AT A SPECIAL PRESS CONFERENCE LAST NIGHT, THE SECRETARY-DESIGNATE ANNOUNCED HE WOULD BE HOLDING REGULAR PHONE-A-THONS TO ASK AVERAGE AMERICANS WHAT SYMBOLS THEY WOULD MOST LIKE TO SEE IN THE CARTER ADMINISTRATION.

TODAY DUANE DELACOURT HELD HIS FIRST SUCH PHONE-A-THON AND NBC NEWS WAS THERE..

HELLO?

HELLO! THIS IS YOUR SECRETARY OF SYMBOLISM!

YEAH, I'D LIKE TO SEE MORE PHONE-A-THONS.

PROP ROOM, RIZZO HERE!

YEAH, RIZZO, THIS IS SECRETARY DELACOURT. I NEED A FAVOR FROM YOU BY NEXT WEEK..

THE BOSS IS GOING TO HAVE A HUMAN RIGHTS BANQUET, AND WE'RE GOING TO NEED SOME TROPHIES. I THINK THOSE LITTLE PLASTIC AND WOOD JOBBIES WILL DO FINE, BUT I WANT SOMETHING APPROPRIATE TO SCREW ON TOP.

WELL, LET'S SEE WHAT I'VE GOT HERE.. I'VE GOT A LITTLE GOLFER.. ..UM..AN EAGLE.. JUSTICE HOLDING UP HER SCALES.. VICTORY WITH A LAUREL WREATH..

NO.. NO.. WHAT ELSE?

HOW ABOUT A LITTLE GUY STRUGGLING WITH HIS CHAINS?

FINE! PERFECT! NOW, I WANT THE INSCRIPTION TO BE SOMETHING FROM GANDHI..

*Eighteen years later, Joanie
continues to receive alumni mailings,
at taxpayers' expense.*

Following Duke's tour of duty, Trudeau was commissioned to paint a portrait of him to hang in the U. S. Embassy.

November 27 **1977**

A Doonesbury Special, an animated film, debuts on NBC. It is later nominated for an Academy Award and wins the Special Jury Prize at the Cannes Film Festival.

Wrote TV critic Marvin Kittman:
"I found it interesting to watch those Walden commune weirdos."

GOOD EVENING. THIS IS THE SCENE IN NEW YORK TONIGHT AS HUNDREDS OF DEMONSTRATORS GATHER OUTSIDE A DINNER FOR THE EMPRESS OF IRAN. ROLAND HEDLEY IS THERE.

HARRY, THERE'S BEEN A SLIGHT DELAY IN THE FESTIVITIES TONIGHT AS WE AWAIT THE LATE ARRIVAL OF PRO-SHAH FORCES HERE AT THE NEW YORK HILTON HOTEL.

BAD WEATHER APPARENTLY DELAYED THE BUSES BRINGING THE SHAH'S RECRUITS TO N.Y., SO OUT OF FAIRNESS, PLANNERS HAVE HELD UP THE BANQUET TO ALLOW COUNTER-DEMONSTRATORS TIME TO TAKE UP THEIR POSITIONS!

LONG LIVE THE SHAH!

..AND HERE THEY COME NOW! LOOKS LIKE THE EVENING'S UNDER WAY, HARRY!

HARRY, I'M TALKING TO A COUPLE OF STUDENTS RIGHT NOW, BUT UNLIKE MOST OF THE FOREIGN DEMONSTRATORS HERE, THESE YOUNG MEN ARE AS AMERICAN AS YOU OR I!

MOREOVER, I AM TOLD THAT THEY ARE STUDENTS OF DR. HENRY KISSINGER, THE FEATURED SPEAKER AT TONIGHT'S DINNER HONORING THE EMPRESS!

GENTLEMEN, TELL ME, WHY ON EARTH ARE YOU WEARING THOSE MASKS? SURELY YOU'RE NOT PROTECTING RELATIVES OR LOVED ONES IN IRAN?

NO, BUT WE'VE GOT MID-TERMS COMING UP, MAN..

WHOA! SAY NO MORE!

WITH THE SERVING OF A PÂTÉ DE FOIE GRAS AND A LIGHT CHABLIS, THE FRIENDS OF EXXON SOCIETY DINNER HONORING THE SHAHBANOU FARRAH IS FINALLY UNDERWAY, HARRY..

DESPITE THE UGLY PROTESTS OUTSIDE, SOME OF OUR BRIGHTEST STARS HAVE TURNED OUT, RANGING FROM VACATIONING NEWSMAN WALTER CRONKITE TO TONIGHT'S BIGGEST SURPRISE, ACTIVIST SHIRLEY MacLAINE!

THE SHAH IS A *MURDERER!* THE SHAH IS A *MURDERER!!*

THE SHAH IS..*AWK!*

WELL, THE SPEECHES HAVE ALREADY BEGUN HERE AT THE HILTON BALLROOM, HARRY..

December 11 **1977**

The Exxon Educational Foundation announces a $100,000 Joanie Caucus Exxon Fellowship Program to aid women over 30 who want to become lawyers.

February 9 1978

In its review of Jimmy Thudpucker's Greatest Hits, the *Buffalo Courier Express* noted, "Thudpucker, who was once part of the solution, is now part of the problem."

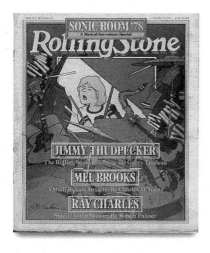

A legend's legend: Jimmy's second *Rolling Stone* cover.

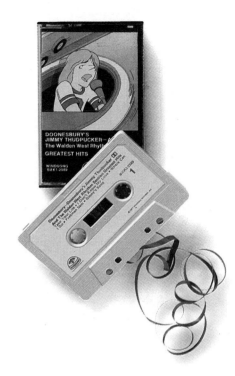

WHN radio host Wizard Wayne
boasts to the New York Daily News:
"I've known Jimmy Thudpucker
most of his life. I used to date
his sister Serena."

Doonesbury urges readers to find out more about "Koreagate" by sending in a newspaper coupon to Speaker of the House Tip O'Neill, who is not pleased when over a dozen sacks of mail arrive. Prior to the strip's release, an O'Neill aide had called Universal Press Syndicate and attempted to stop its publication.

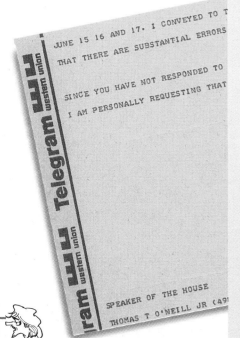

Q ···· What's the deal with Zonker's beach in Malibu?

A ···· Well, it's not really a beach. It's a beach accessway. In the late 70s, the California Coastal Commission liberated a number of public beaches that had been, in effect, privatized by residents who owned property in front of them. Naturally, the new access routes were not popular with folks accustomed to thinking of the beaches as their own, and the redwood sign marking the Zonker Harris Memorial Accessway was vandalized within 24 hours.

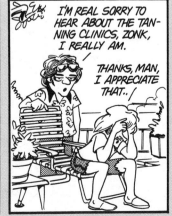

—GEORGE HAMILTON

The Republican caucus of the Virginia General Assembly censures Trudeau for his satirical treatment of Senator John Warner and his wife Elizabeth Taylor. The 28 Republicans vote unanimously to express their "outrage and indignation." Fumed the motion's sponsor, State Senator Wiley Mitchell, "I don't think we should sit placidly by and let the gnomes of the world run over us without expressing indignation."

When the *Washington Post* suspends *Doonesbury*, the strip is read on talk shows and TV news programs, and even appears in the White House News Summary "as a service to our readers." Jody Powell tells a White House press briefing that he might ask the Justice Department to look into the strip's disappearance.

WHAT SORT OF SWAY DOES "TED" HAVE OVER HIS FOLLOWERS? I ASKED LIBERAL CONGRESSMAN BART SVIGALS, WHO FLED WASHINGTON DURING LAST YEAR'S OUTBREAK OF TAX-CUT FEVER..

CONGRESSMAN, YOU'VE BEEN IN SELF-IMPOSED EXILE NOW FOR OVER A YEAR, RIGHT?

THAT'S CORRECT, ROLLIE. EVER SINCE THE ROTH-KEMP BILL WAS INTRODUCED.

WOULD YOU RETURN TO CONGRESS IF SENATOR KENNEDY ASKED YOU TO?

YES, I WOULD. I WOULD DO ANYTHING FOR THE MAN.

WOULD YOU.. WOULD YOU OVERSPEND FOR HIM?

LAVISHLY. WITHOUT HESITATION.

COMPASSION. JUSTICE. A FAIR SHAKE. THESE ARE THE PROFESSED GOALS OF THE KENNEDY "CULT OF CONSCIENCE."

AND YET, FOR ALL THE EGALITARIAN POSTURING OF THE LIBERALS, GATHERING SIGNS INDICATE THAT WITHIN THE CULT ITSELF, SOME ARE MORE EQUAL THAN OTHERS!

ABC NEWS HAS JUST LEARNED OF THE EXISTENCE OF AN INNER ELITE, A TIGHTLY-KNIT CADRE OF LOYALISTS SO CLOSE TO "TED" THAT THEY'RE ACTUALLY RELATED TO HIM.

REFERRED TO AS THE KENNEDY "CLAN," THEIR EXACT NUMBER IS UNKNOWN..

THE KENNEDY "CLAN." HEIRS TO A POWERFUL LIBERAL LEGACY, THEY ASPIRE FANATICALLY TO A STATE OF TOTAL GRACE.

RESTRICTED DURING THE SUMMER MONTHS TO A FAMILY "COMPOUND," CLAN MEMBERS ARE FORCED TO PRACTICE THEIR BACKHANDS, GROW LONG, UNKEMPT HAIR, AND POSE FOR ENDLESS GROUP PHOTOGRAPHS.

LATER, IN THE FALL, YOUNGER CLAN MEMBERS ARE SENT AWAY TO THE RIGORS OF BOARDING SCHOOL, WHILE OLDER MEMBERS ARE CONFINED TO HARVARD.

DISCIPLINE IS TIGHT. ONLY AFTER THEY HAVE COMPLETED THEIR STUDIES MAY THEY RUN FOR OFFICE.

> **"** I, the Mayor of the District of Columbia, do hereby proclaim Monday, June 25, 1979, as 'Doonesbury Day' in Washington, D.C., and call upon all of the people of our city to join with me in welcoming the reappearance of *Doonesbury* and in participating in appropriate ceremonies during this day, 'Doonesbury Day' in our Nation's Capital. **"**

— MARION BARRY, JR.

Mistaking Zeke for a raccoon

Awarded to G. B. Trudeau, age 12,
for achievement in the prone position.

Panel 1: WE'RE BACK TALKING WITH DR. ALI MAHDAVI, '74, ON LEAVE FROM THE IRANIAN REVOLUTIONARY TRIBUNAL, AND HERE ON CAMPUS FOR HIS FIFTH REUNION!

Panel 2: DR. MAHDAVI, FOR OVER A YEAR NOW, AMERICANS HAVE BEEN HEARING ABOUT THE DARK, SINISTER SIDE OF IRAN'S BEARDED HOLY MAN.

Panel 3: I WONDER IF YOU COULD TELL US SOMETHING OF THE OTHER SIDE, THE HUMAN SIDE.. / SUCH AS?

Panel 4: WELL, LIKE WHAT DO BEARDED HOLY MEN HAVE FOR BREAKFAST? / SHAHS. IS THIS GOING TO TAKE LONG?

Panel 5: DR. MAHDAVI, HOW DO YOU RESPOND TO CRITICISM THAT YOUR NEW REVOLUTIONARY GOVERNMENT IS RAPIDLY BECOMING THE WORSE OF TWO EVILS?

Panel 6: IT HAS BEEN CHARGED, FOR INSTANCE, THAT THE AYATOLLAH'S ISLAMIC REPUBLIC IS, IN EFFECT, RETURNING IRAN TO THE 14TH CENTURY!

Panel 7: WELL, YES, THAT WAS THE ORIGINAL PLAN, BUT IT IS ENTIRELY POSSIBLE THERE WILL BE SOME COMPROMISE ON THE EXACT ERA.

Panel 8: YOU MEAN, THERE'S A NEW TARGET DATE? / YES, SOME OF US ARE TRYING TO GET IT MOVED UP TO THE AGE OF VOLTAIRE.

Panel 9: AS YOU KNOW, DR. MAHDAVI, IN RECENT WEEKS, THERE HAS BEEN AN OUTPOURING OF PROTEST FROM IRANIAN WOMEN OVER THE ALL-COVERING "CHADOR," WHICH THEY SEE AS A SYMBOL OF ISLAMIC SEXISM.

Panel 10: WILL THE AYATOLLAH RESPOND TO THIS NEW.. / IT HAS ALREADY BEEN RESOLVED. THE RULE ABOUT THE CHADOR WAS BEING TAKEN TOO LITERALLY.

Panel 11: THE AYATOLLAH DOES NOT DISAPPROVE OF OTHER FORMS OF DRESS, AS LONG AS THEY ARE MODEST. WHAT HE DOES OBJECT TO ARE SKIRTS AND GOWNS, THE GARMENTS OF PROSTITUTES!

Panel 12: I SEE. HOW ABOUT THE ANNIE HALL LOOK? / IF WORN WITH A VEIL, FINE.

A crate of original *Doonesbury* drawings is stolen from the office of Trudeau's answering service, only to be recovered in a police raid on the Sunshine Girls Escort Service in Hamden, Connecticut. Sunshine's unlucky social director is subsequently convicted of first-degree larceny, largely on the strength of Trudeau's ability to recognize his own work in court.

The perpetrator was nabbed at the Canadian border.

CLASS OF 1979. I GREET YOU ON THE OCCASION OF MY TENTH COMMENCEMENT ADDRESS TO THE GRADUATING CLASS OF THIS UNIVERSITY..

I NEED NOT TELL YOU IT HAS BEEN A REMARKABLE DECADE. AND AS THE LAST CLASS TO GRADUATE IN THE SEVENTIES, IT IS FITTING THAT YOU ARE NO LESS REMARKABLE.

AS YOU KNOW, A RECORD NUMBER OF YOU HAVE BEEN ACCEPTED AT TOP LAW AND MEDICAL SCHOOLS. MANY OTHERS HAVE RECEIVED PRESTIGIOUS AWARDS AND FELLOWSHIPS FOR STUDY ABROAD.

AM I PROUD OF YOU? DO I TAKE MORE THAN ORDINARY PLEASURE IN THIS ASTONISHING RECORD?

BY WAY OF ANSWER, I WOULD LIKE TO SHARE WITH YOU THE OPENING WORDS OF MY GRADUATION SPEECH TO THE CLASS OF 1970..

"ATTENTION: WILL THE STUDENTS WHO TRASHED MY OFFICE LAST NIGHT PLEASE RETURN THE DIPLOMAS?"

GBTrudeau

West Coast papers drop a sequence linking Governor Jerry Brown to alleged underworld figure Sidney Korshak. In a nice touch, the only papers outside of California to kill the strip are located in Reno and Las Vegas.

BUILD WE MUST!

BOY, I HAD A **CORKER** OF A DREAM LAST NIGHT, GANG!

HERE WE GO AGAIN..

WHAT WAS IT ABOUT, ELLIE?

WELL, IT WAS PART OF A CONTINUING SERIES ABOUT SISTERHOOD..

IN IT, I DREAMT THAT THE EQUAL RIGHTS AMENDMENT WAS PASSED UNANIMOUSLY BY ALL FIFTY STATES!

YOU WERE DREAMING, ALL RIGHT.

ANYTHING ELSE?

YEAH. JUST BEFORE I WOKE UP, THERE WAS FULL COMPLIANCE ACROSS THE LAND!

WOW.. YOU SURE HAVE INTERESTING DREAMS, ELLIE.

THANKS, LILLY. WHAT DO YOU DREAM ABOUT, HOWARD?

MY NEXT TWINKIE.

HEY, ME, TOO! DO YOU SUCK THE CREAMY PART OUT FIRST?

GBTrudeau

1980~1984

"Anybody who can draw bad pictures of the White House four times in a row and succeed knows something I don't."

—AL CAPP, CREATOR OF L'IL ABNER

Q •••• Were you shocked when *The Wall Street Journal* turned over its entire New Year's Day op-ed page to reprinting your *fin-de-decade* strips?

A •••• Well, there was a little soul-searching, but the fact was, taken as a whole, the series did reveal a markedly conservative perspective on a wide variety of social issues. And that was before I had children. My guess is that the *Journal* reprinted it as a welcome turn of events, although it's also possible they had nothing else to run that day.

*A salute to the '70s
— a kidney stone
of a decade.*

The presidential candidacy of Republican Congressman John Anderson receives an unexpected boost through the attentions of Mike Doonesbury. At first Anderson calls the coverage "nifty," but later in the campaign, after Barbara Bush dubs him "the *Doonesbury* candidate," Anderson has second thoughts.

Confided the candidate's wife, Keke, to Playboy, *"With Garry Trudeau, you had the most respected advance man in politics."*

NOW MORE THAN EVER, WE MUST NOT PERMIT OURSELVES TO BE OVERCOME WITH A NEW MISSILE MADNESS, A MINDLESS RENEWAL OF UNRESTRICTED COMPETITION.

BEFORE IT IS TOO LATE, WE MUST MOVE TO RATIFY SALT. SALT IS NOT A UNILATERAL FAVOR WE ARE DOING THE SOVIET UNION; WE SHOULD NOT BE PENALIZING OURSELVES FOR SOVIET BEHAVIOR!

EXCUSE ME, CONGRESSMAN ANDERSON, BUT ARE YOU **SURE** YOU'RE A REPUBLICAN? YOU SURE DON'T **SOUND** LIKE A REPUBLICAN!

GREAT.

HEY, BUT WHAT DO I KNOW? I'M A DEMOCRAT.

YES, IT WILL TAKE MORE THAN HORTATORY EXPRESSIONS ABOUT LEADERSHIP TO RESTORE OUR FLAGGING NATIONAL FORTUNES. THAT'S WHY I'M RUNNING AND THAT'S WHY I NEED YOUR SUPPORT!

BRAVO! YEAA!

CLAP! CLAP! CLAP!

WE WANT ANDERSON! WE WANT ANDERSON!

STOMP! STOMP!

THANK YOU. COULD YOU TELL ME HOW TO GET TO THE BUS STATION?

SURE. DO YOU NEED A LIFT?

ZONK? HI, IT'S MIKE. LISTEN, I'M DOWN AT THE BUS STATION..

ROCHES

CONGRESSMAN ANDERSON MISSED HIS BUS, SO I'M GOING TO DRIVE HIM UP TO CONCORD.

CONCORD? THAT'S FIVE HOURS!

ROCHES

I KNOW, BUT HE'S A GOOD GUY, AND HE NEEDS THE LIFT. ALSO, HE SAID I COULD ADVANCE FOR HIM IF I WANTED TO.

ADVANCE FOR HIM? WHAT DOES HE MEAN BY ADVANCE?

ROCHES

CONGRESSMAN? WHAT DO YOU MEAN BY ADVANCE?

IN MY CASE, IT MEANS YOU GET OUT OF THE CAR FIRST.

66 *I don't regard* Doonesbury *as the apotheosis of what the John Anderson campaign is all about.* 99

— JOHN ANDERSON

137

I PROPOSE WE QUIETLY DISBAND AT HALF-TIME.

Q **·····** Given its volatile nature, the hostage crisis in Iran must have been a difficult subject for cartoonists.

A **·····** It was. Early on, I had to recall and retool material. Oddly enough — considering how much I was writing about the crisis — *Doonesbury* was one of the few things the Iranian students failed to censor from the hostages' reading material. They had made a familiar assumption — that nothing of consequence could be found in a comic strip.

Panel 1: I REALLY SHOULDN'T BE DRIVING YOU INTO TEHRAN WITHOUT A WORK ORDER FROM THE IMAM. I COULD GET MY HANDS CHOPPED OFF.

Panel 2: WELL, I APPRECIATE YOUR ACCEPTING A BRIBE. I REALLY DO. IT'S BEEN A WHILE. WE DON'T GET TOO MANY WESTERNERS IN TOWN ANYMORE.

Panel 3: THE ONLY AMERICANS WE'VE SEEN IN MONTHS ARE THE LIARS AND DEMONS OF THE U.S. PRESS. YOU HAIL FROM THE GREAT SATAN YOURSELF, RIGHT?

Panel 4: UH.. RIGHT. NEW YORK, ACTUALLY. I CAN ALWAYS TELL. HOW LONG YOU BEEN WORKING FOR THE CIA?

Panel 5: YES? REVEREND SLOAN, I'M DR. ALI MAHDAVI, I'M FROM THE REVOLUTIONARY COUNCIL.

Panel 6: AT LAST! I WAS BEGINNING TO THINK I'D BEEN FORGOTTEN. NOT AT ALL. MAY I COME IN?

Panel 7: WHY, OF COURSE, DR. MAHDAVI! PLEASE! I CAN'T STAY LONG. I LEFT MY MOB OUTSIDE.

Panel 8: DEATH TO CARTER! DEATH TO CARTER! YOU.. UH.. HAVE YOUR OWN MOB? YES. WE'RE ON OUR WAY TO A FUNERAL.

Panel 9: BUT YOU STILL HAVEN'T SAID WHEN I CAN SEE THE HOSTAGES, DR. MAHDAVI. ALL IN GOOD TIME, FATHER, ALL IN GOOD TIME.

Panel 10: PERHAPS IF I COULD SPEAK TO SOMEONE IN AUTHORITY.. AUTHORITY? MY DEAR REVEREND, I AM THE AUTHORITY!

Panel 11: THE STUDENTS HAVE BEEN TOLD BY THE IMAM HIMSELF THEY ARE TO ANSWER TO ME! THE WELL-BEING OF THE HOSTAGES IS **COMPLETELY** IN MY HANDS!

Panel 12: GREAT, ANY IDEA WHERE THEY ARE? I'M WORKING ON IT. LOOK, WHY DON'T YOU TAKE IN SOME OF THE SIGHTS?

> 66 Doonesbury *got the message through that the U.S. is very much aware of its citizens, now in the tenth week of imprisonment.* 99

— WILLIAM F. KEOGH, JR.
on the strips he received while in captivity

"Gotta run — my government's collapsing."

GOOD EVENING FROM LONDON. TODAY NEAR KABUL, AFGHAN REBELS STAGED ANOTHER STUNNING RAID ON A SOVIET ENCAMPMENT OUTSIDE THE TROUBLED CAPITAL...

WHO ARE THESE PLUCKY CHAMPIONS OF AFGHAN INDEPENDENCE? WHAT DRIVES THEM TO FIGHT ON AGAINST OVERWHELMING ODDS? AT GREAT PERSONAL RISK, OUR MAN ROLAND HEDLEY SET OUT TO FIND THE ANSWERS.

UNSHAVEN AND CLAD IN THE INDIGENOUS GARB OF AN AFGHAN MOUNTAINEER, HEDLEY SLIPPED UNNOTICED ACROSS THE AFGHAN BORDER AND FILED THE FOLLOWING REPORT.

ROLLIE, I'M STILL GETTING GLARE FROM YOUR NOSE.

THREE.. TWO.. ONE!

GOOD EVENING FROM KHYBER PASS.

..AND SO GREAT IS THE DANGER OF BEING FIRED ON BY THE SOVIET TROOPS BELOW, IT'LL BE A MIRACLE IF THIS EXCLUSIVE REPORT EVER GETS OUT. IN KHYBER PASS, THIS IS ROLAND HEDLEY.

OKAY, I THINK WE FINALLY GOT A KEEPER.

WELL DONE, LADS!

NEED ANYTHING ELSE?

YEAH, WHY DON'T YOU GO DOWN THE HILL AND GET A SHOT OF ME LOOKING OVER THE VALLEY?

I THOUGHT YOU SAID THERE WERE RUSSIANS DOWN THERE.

OH, HELL, THEY WON'T BOTHER YOU. YOU'RE PRESS.

HELLO? HELLO, SIR?

HELLO, I WONDER IF I COULD HAVE A FEW WORDS WITH YOU.

WAIT! COME BACK! I MEAN YOU NO HARM!

I'M JUST A SIMPLE MOUNTAINEER LIKE YOURSELF!

FORGET IT, MAN. NONE OF THESE RAG-HEADS SPEAK AMERICAN ANYWAY.

HELLO? HELLO, UP THERE?

WHO IS IT?

WE'RE FRIENDS! WE MEAN YOU NO HARM!

WHO ARE YOU?

WE'RE JOURNALISTS! WE WANT TO TALK! WE'RE FROM TELEVISION, AMERICAN TELEVISION.

CBS OR NBC?

UH.. ABC. BUT WE'RE NUMBER TWO NOW.

MR. MESHAK, I CERTAINLY APPRECIATE YOUR LETTING ABC NEWS TAKE AN UP-CLOSE CLOSE-UP OF LIFE IN A REBEL CAMP!

NO PROBLEM. WHERE'S YOUR CREW?

THEY'RE BRINGING UP THE EQUIPMENT. THEY SHOULD BE HERE SHORTLY.

GOOD. I WANT TO DO THE INTERVIEW RIGHT AWAY.

UH.. RIGHT AWAY?

YES. DOES THIS PRESENT A PROBLEM?

WELL, FRANKLY, I WAS HOPING YOU'D BE DRESSED IN COLORFUL NATIVE GARB.

OH. WELL, MAYBE I COULD BORROW YOURS.

THIS IS ROLAND HEDLEY AND I'M STANDING BY LIVE AND INCOGNITO BEHIND INSURGENT LINES WITH AFGHAN REBEL LEADER BABRAK MESHAK..

ROLLIE, THIS IS BARBARA WALTERS IN NEW YORK. CAN YOU HEAR ME?

YES, BARBARA. GO AHEAD.

MR. MESHAK, COULD YOU TELL ABC EXCLUSIVELY WHAT YOUR PLANS ARE?

MR. MESHAK, BARBARA WALTERS WOULD LIKE TO KNOW WHAT YOUR PLANS ARE?

WHO'S BARBARA WALTERS?

HE'S AN IGNORANT SAVAGE, BARBARA. PAY NO MIND.

GB Trudeau

More than two dozen newspapers drop "The Mysterious World of Reagan's Brain," a week-long sequence that runs on the eve of the 1980 election. One of those papers, *The Indianapolis Star*, receives 850 calls of protest before it agrees to reinstate the strip. Opines the Rochester *Times-Union*, "Any voters who might be influenced by something they read on the comic page probably shouldn't be voting."

OKAY, PEOPLE, QUIET ON THE SET, PLEASE!

SCENE ONE.. TAKE ONE!

"MR. REAGAN GOES TO WASHINGTON"

SCENE 1   TAKE 1

ACTION!

..AND WITH KEY SECOND-LEVEL POSTS STILL UN-FILLED, THE TRANSITION PERIOD HAS BY NO MEANS ENDED WITH RONALD REAGAN'S SWEARING-IN CEREMONIES.

ON ANOTHER FRONT, HOWEVER, THE REAGANS SEEM TO HAVE GOTTEN OFF TO A ROARING START..

ONLY MINUTES AFTER THE INAUGURATION, MRS. REAGAN WAS WHISKED TO THE WHITE HOUSE WHERE SHE QUICKLY ASSUMED CONTROL OF THE HOUSE-HOLD FROM THE FORM-ER FIRST LADY.

WHAT DO YOU WANT? GET OUT! IT'S **MINE** NOW!

UM..SORRY, I JUST FORGOT MY PURSE.

MRS. REAGAN, WHEN DID YOU FIRST ACQUIRE YOUR HAND-GUN?

IT WAS BACK WHEN RONNIE WAS TOURING THE COUNTRY FOR G.E.

HOLLYWOOD WAS JUST SWARMING WITH COMMUNISTS IN THOSE DAYS, AND RONNIE FELT I SHOULDN'T BE ALONE IN THE HOUSE WITH-OUT PROTEC-TION.

BUT IT'S NO BIG DEAL. IT'S JUST THIS TINY LITTLE THING WITH VERY PRETTY MOTHER-OF-PEARL INLAY AND LITTLE DAISIES ETCHED ON THE BARREL.

AND WHAT DOES IT SHOOT?

TEENY-WEENY, LADY-LIKE BULLETS.

66 *I don't read Garry Trudeau.* 99

— NANCY REAGAN

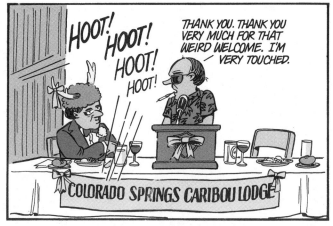

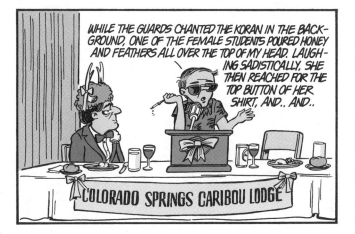

Last seen before an Iranian firing squad on September 7, 1979, Uncle Duke is released, after the other 52 American hostages, from captivity. Cheers the Lexington, Ky. *Herald*, "Welcome home, well done — whatever it was you did over there."

Reported UPI, "Uncle Duke is alive and well and probably stoned somewhere in Wiesbaden, Germany."

August 19 **1981**

The Detroit Free Press announces the Zonker Harris Testimonial Tan-Off. Cash prizes total $210.

He came to tan: Zonker takes his event at the 1981 Gerald R. Ford Pro-am Summer Biathlon.

ERRATA:
THE WEDDING IS ON THURSDAY, JUNE 18. THE NAME OF THE BRIDEGOON IS "RICK," NOT "BICK".

Thanks

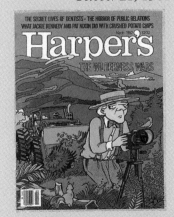

Ansel Adams called the aging agitator: "Unusual... someone to watch for..."

Neither did little boys.

159

In the heartland, a heart to heart.

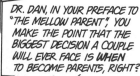

Panel 1: DAN, ONE OF THE MOST FASCINATING CHAPTERS OF YOUR BOOK IS ENTITLED "QUALITY TIME." I WONDER IF YOU COULD EXPLAIN THE QUALITY TIME CONCEPT TO US.

Panel 2: FOR SURE, MARK. QUALITY TIME IS THE KIND OF TIME YOU SPEND WITH YOUR KIDS IF YOU'RE REALLY TOO PRESSED TO GIVE THEM THE MORE TRADITIONAL QUANTITY TIME!

Panel 3: BY GIVING A CHILD QUALITY TIME, THAT IS, HIGHLY CONCENTRATED DOSAGES OF FOCUSED ATTENTION, THE BUSY PARENT CAN SHAVE VALUABLE HOURS OFF THE TIME REQUIRED TO IMPACT HIS CHILD'S DEVELOPMENT.

Panel 4: SO QUALITY TIME IS BASICALLY A TIME-SAVER. / RIGHT. IT WORKS WITH OLD PEOPLE, TOO, BY THE WAY.

Panel 5: DAN, IN YOUR BOOK YOU CLAIM THAT A MAJOR PROBLEM FOR THE MELLOW PARENT IS DESIGNER JEANS. / THAT'S RIGHT, MARK. DESIGNER JEANS ARE TEARING A LOT OF FAMILIES APART.

Panel 6: BECAUSE OF BROOKE SHIELDS AND ALL THE T.V. ADS, KIDS TODAY ARE CLAMORING FOR STATUS JEANS. UNFORTUNATELY, THEY GROW OUT OF THEM QUICKLY, SO MANY PARENTS DON'T THINK THEY'RE WORTH THE MONEY.

Panel 7: SO WHICH SIDE OF THE ISSUE DO YOU COME DOWN ON, DAN? / I'M PRO-JEANS, MARK. KIDS WILL BE JUDGED ON THEIR JEANS ALL THEIR LIVES. PARENTS WHO SKIMP ON JEANS GIVE THEIR CHILDREN A SOCIAL HANDICAP!

Panel 8: HOW ABOUT DESIGNER WATER? SAME THING? / ABSOLUTELY. THE KID WHO DOESN'T HAVE PERRIER IN HIS LUNCHPAIL COULD MISS THE BOAT!

Panel 9: DR. DAN, ONE OF THE THINGS YOU RECOMMEND TO NEW PARENTS IS A VIDEO-CASSETTE RECORDING SYSTEM, RIGHT? / THAT'S RIGHT, MARK. I FEEL THAT VIDEO WILL BE THE FAMILY SCRAPBOOK OF THE EIGHTIES!

Panel 10: WITH A GOOD PORTABLE SYSTEM, YOU'LL BE ABLE TO CAPTURE ALL THOSE EARLY MOMENTS YOU'LL TREASURE FOR YEARS TO COME, INCLUDING THE ACTUAL MOMENT OF BIRTH!

Panel 11: BIRTH? YOU'RE JOKING! / NOT AT ALL. MOST DELIVERY ROOMS ARE WELL-LIT, SO ALL YOU DO IS POP IN A CASSETTE AND YOU'LL HAVE A TAPE OF JUNIOR YOU'LL WANT TO SHOW OVER AND OVER AGAIN!

Panel 12: UM.. LIKE WHEN? / WELL, LIKE AT HIS BIRTHDAY PARTIES! HIS LITTLE FRIENDS WILL HOWL!

February 7 **1982**

In response to a suicide threat by EPA staffer and *Doonesbury* character Ted Simpson, the agency issues an internal memo outlining new "security measures" for windows and ledges.

YES.. RICK.

MR. PRESIDENT, I WONDER IF YOU COULD ADDRESS YOUR GROWING PROBLEM OF MISSTATEMENTS DURING PRESS CONFERENCES.

WELL, NOW, I WAS HOPING YOU FELLAHS WOULD ASK ME THAT. I HAVE HERE A SPECIAL ENVELOPE CONTAINING DOCUMENTATION PROVING THAT 9 OF MY LAST 14 MISSTATEMENTS HAD A GRAIN OF TRUTH TO THEM.

WHICH CONFERENCES WOULD THAT COVER, SIR?

LET'S SEE.. I THINK IT'S JANUARY 21 AND FEBRUARY 14.

UM.. YOU MEAN JANUARY 19 AND FEBRUARY 18, DON'T YOU, SIR?

WELL, YES, BUT THERE YOU GO AGAIN, RICK. THE IMPORTANT THING TO THE AMERICAN PEOPLE IS THAT I WAS RIGHT ON THOSE FACTS 10 OUT OF 14 TIMES. I WAS BATTING OVER .900!

LET ME JUST EXPLAIN MY SUCCESS RATE IN TERMS EVERYONE CAN UNDERSTAND..

OH, NO..

HE'S DOING IT AGAIN!

UH.. SIR, THAT WON'T BE NECESSARY..

IF I TAKE TWO GOLF BALLS AND CUT THEM IN HALF..

SOMEBODY **STOP** HIM! HE'S GOING OVER OUR HEADS DIRECTLY TO THE PEOPLE!

SIR? SIR?

— JOHN LEONARD
reviewing a Doonesbury *book in* The New York Times

Trudeau announces a 20-month leave of absence, claiming that "investigative cartooning is a young man's game." Farewell editorials appear across the country. Laments former President Jimmy Carter, "I'm heartbroken."

Panel 1: IT'S TRUE, B.D.! GETTING IN SHAPE AND POLITICAL ACTIVISM ARE RELATED! / WHAT GARBAGE! WERE THE SPARTANS POLITICALLY ACTIVE? ARE THE CINCINNATI BENGALS?

Panel 2: IF YOU LOOK AT YOUR HISTORY, ALL THE PEOPLE WHO PROMOTED PHYSICAL FITNESS THROUGH THE AGES HAVE BEEN CONSERVATIVE. BELIEVE ME, LIBERALS KNOW NOTHING ABOUT GETTING IN SHAPE, ESPECIALLY LADY LIBERALS!

Panel 3: OH, YEAH? / YEAH!

Panel 4: WHAT ABOUT THE BIKINI SCENE IN "GOLDEN POND"? / THAT WAS ALL SPECIAL EFFECTS! JEEZ, BOOPSIE, SOMETIMES YOU CAN BE SO GULLIBLE!

Panel 5: JOB INTERVIEWS? YOU'RE ACTUALLY SIGNING UP FOR JOB INTERVIEWS? / WE'RE SENIORS, ZONK. WHAT OTHER CHOICE DO WE HAVE?

Panel 6: BUT I DON'T KNOW THE FIRST THING ABOUT JOB INTERVIEWS! I'D BE EATEN ALIVE! / NO, YOU WOULDN'T, ZONK..

Panel 7: IT'S REALLY NO BIG DEAL. YOU JUST TALK TO THE RECRUITER FOR TWENTY MINUTES OR SO. ALL YOU HAVE TO DO IS BE YOURSELF.

Panel 8: BUT.. BUT WHAT IF THEY OFFER ME A JOB? / WELL, YOU ALWAYS RUN THAT RISK.

Panel 9: NAME? / HARRIS, ZONKER.

Panel 10: WHICH COMPANIES ARE YOU INTERESTED IN INTERVIEWING WITH? / DEPENDS. WHAT HAVE YOU GOT?

Panel 11: MR. HARRIS, THERE ARE OVER 200 COMPANIES RECRUITING ON CAMPUS. WHAT ARE YOUR GENERAL AREAS OF INTEREST? / AERODYNAMICS. DESIGNER JEANS. ROOFING SUPPLIES. THAT SORT OF THING.

Panel 12: WHAT SORT OF THING? / YOU KNOW, LIQUIDITY. POINT-OF-SALE. MARGIN ACCOUNTS. FAST LANE. / CAREFUL, ZONK. YOU'LL PEAK BEFORE THE INTERVIEWS.

> 66 *It was cold as holy hell in that water. I wish it had been done with special effects.* 99

—JANE FONDA
*responding to "special effects" claim
in Doonesbury*

167

November 9 **1982**

Zonker Harris receives one vote for the governorship in Illinois.

*After twelve years,
the Class of '83 moves on.*

An American runner, jogging through Moscow wearing a Zonker T-shirt, is stopped several times by Russians who ask if the T-shirt likeness is a caricature of Trotsky. They said with evident political concern, "You know, Trotsky is not accepted over here." A few, with a different perception, asked, "Is that really Lenin on the American T-shirt?"

January 2 **1983**

Doonesbury ceases publication. The Wisconsin State Assembly issues a declaration pleading for "public calm in the face of this grave crisis."

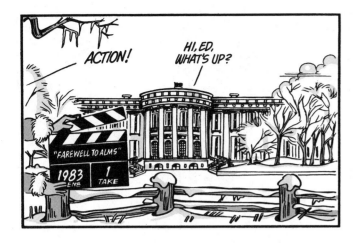

"Doonesbury, A Musical" opened at Broadway's Biltmore Theater on November 21, 1983, earning Grammy and Drama Desk Award nominations.

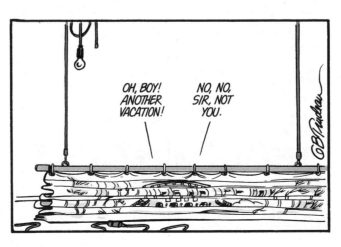

Doonesbury returns to syndication. The Wisconsin Assembly repeals its 20-month state of emergency.

MIKE, HERE'S THE POOP. OUR TOP ACCOUNT HAS JUST HANDED US A RUSH CAMPAIGN, AND I NEED A YOUNG COMER WHO CAN GET IT ON TRACK FAST. CASS HERE SAYS THAT YOU'RE MY MAN!

WELL, SIR, I'LL DO MY BEST NOT TO LET YOU DOWN. I'M VERY EXCITED ABOUT BEING A COPYWRITER, AND I'M ANXIOUS TO GET GOING!

AS LONG AS I'M SELLING SOMETHING I BELIEVE IN, I'LL GIVE YOU EVERYTHING I'VE GOT!

GREAT. I WANT YOU TO SELL RONALD REAGAN TO BLACK VOTERS.

I CAN'T STAND IT..

I SEE A CALVIN KLEIN APPROACH. RECLINING BLACK TEENAGERS TALKING ABOUT THEIR FIRST JOBS.

YOU WANT ME TO WORK ON A SPOT FOR THE REAGAN CAMPAIGN?

THAT'S RIGHT. AN APPEAL TO BLACK VOTERS.

BLACK VOTERS? THAT'S GREAT! HEE, HEE!.. SERIOUSLY?

SERIOUSLY.

HEH..

THIS IS A TEST, RIGHT? TO SEE IF I HAVE ANY SHAME?

CAREFUL, MIKE..

WHAT'S THE PROBLEM, SON?

HOW DID IT GO? WELL, LET ME TELL YOU. FIRST, I MISSED MY TRAIN AND I WAS AN HOUR LATE. THEN MY OFFICE WASN'T READY. THEN THE RECEPTIONIST MADE A MAJOR PASS AT ME.

THEN, TO TOP IT OFF, I WAS INFORMED THAT MY FIRST ASSIGNMENT IS TO PREPARE A REAGAN CAMPAIGN SPOT AIMED AT BLACK VOTERS. CAN YOU BELIEVE IT?

NEVER MIND THAT THE WHOLE IDEA IS PREPOSTEROUS. WHAT REALLY WORRIES ME IS THAT I ACCEPTED, THAT I'M ALREADY BEGINNING TO LOSE THE COURAGE OF MY CONVICTIONS.

DOES IT WORRY YOU, TOO, J.J.?

NOT NEARLY AS MUCH AS THE RECEPTIONIST.

173

Q .... You got hammered a lot for your Reagan strips during the 1984 election. Were you surprised?

A .... Yes, but I shouldn't have been. By that time, Reagan was so universally regarded as "nice" that even the mildest criticism of him was judged churlish and mean-spirited. Obviously Reagan's unique blend of manly jingoism and sunny cluelessness had been a tonic for a nation yearning to feel good about itself again. But his presidency always reminded me of a remark made by a woman to Heywood Broun following Secretariat's victory in the Triple Crown. After the trauma of Vietnam and Watergate, she said, Secretariat had "restored her faith in humanity." I like to think Reagan was the Secretariat of the eighties.

OKAY, THIS IS JUST ONE POSSIBILITY. I THOUGHT I'D TRY TO PLAY UP HIS MANLY IMAGE WITH A SURREAL, VIDEO APPROACH..

GOOD DIRECTION!

WE OPEN ON A ROCK CONCERT WITH A MULTI-RACIAL BAND PLAYING IN FRONT OF A HUGE AMERICAN FLAG. AS BLINDING FIREWORKS ERUPT, THE FLAG LIFTS TO REVEAL A LONG, WHITE STAIRCASE!

STANDING AT THE TOP IS REAGAN. HE'S DRESSED IN JEANS AND AN OPEN SHIRT. AS A THOUSAND TEENAGERS SCREAM "PEACE THROUGH STRENGTH," HE STARTS DOWN THE STAIRS.

SUDDENLY, HIS HAIR CATCHES FIRE.

BUT HE DOESN'T FLINCH! LOVE IT!

YOU KNOW, I ALWAYS THOUGHT HIS HAIR LOOKED FLAMMABLE.

GOOD EVENING. VICE PRESIDENT GEORGE BUSH'S MANHOOD PROBLEM SURFACED AGAIN TODAY, AS CONCERN OVER HIS LACK OF POLITICAL COURAGE CONTINUED TO GROW.

CAMPAIGN OFFICIALS, ALARMED BY REACTION TO BUSH'S NUMEROUS POLICY REVERSALS, HAVE PERSUADED HIM TO TAKE SWIFT ACTION TO PREVENT FURTHER EROSION OF HIS BELIEFS.

ACCORDINGLY, IN A WHITE HOUSE CEREMONY TODAY, BUSH WILL FORMALLY PLACE HIS EMBATTLED MANHOOD IN A BLIND TRUST.

IT WILL BE RESTORED TO HIM ONLY IN TIMES OF NATIONAL EMERGENCY.

THE ECONOMY. ERA. ABORTION. DEFICITS. THESE ARE JUST SOME OF THE ISSUES GEORGE BUSH HAS REVERSED HIMSELF ON TO BECOME A REAGAN TEAM PLAYER.

TO SHELTER WHAT REMAINS OF HIS CONVICTIONS, BUSH IS ABOUT TO FORMALLY PLACE HIS POLITICAL MANHOOD IN A BLIND TRUST. AND HERE COMES THE VICE PRESIDENT NOW!

MR. VICE PRESIDENT! MR. VICE PRESIDENT!

YES.. ROLAND?

SIR, WILL YOUR MANHOOD BE EARNING INTEREST?

VERY LITTLE. THERE'S NOT THAT MUCH CAPITAL.

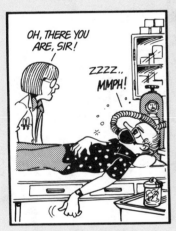

Escondido Times-Advocate editor Will Corbin drops *Doonesbury*, writing, "If it's the only basis upon which a decision to buy this newspaper is made, then I might as well be selling shoes."

Escondido Times-Advocate editor Will Corbin selling shoes.

BEFORE I INTRODUCE THE INAUGURAL SPEAKER, A FEW WORDS. IN THE MONTHS AHEAD, YOU WILL ALL STUDY MEDICINE. YOU WILL PLAY GOLF. YOU WILL LEARN ABOUT TAX SHELTERS. IN SHORT, YOU WILL BECOME DOCTORS!

BUT COME FEBRUARY, LADIES AND GENTLEMEN, YOU WILL DO THE MOST IMPORTANT THING YOU'LL EVER DO IN YOUR LIVES! YOU WILL MEET ST. GEORGE'S IN GRENADA, AND YOU WILL DESTROY THEM IN VOLLEYBALL!

YEAAA!

CLAP!
CLAP!
CLAP!
CLAP!

GRENADA SUCKS EGGS! GRENADA SUCKS EGGS!

POINT SPREAD CITY!

THEY SURE HAVE A LOT OF SCHOOL SPIRIT, SIR.

BEAT ST. GEORGE! BEAT ST. GEORGE!

OKAY, OKAY. SETTLE DOWN!

NOW, REMEMBER, PEOPLE, NO PAIN, NO GAIN! I WANT YOU OUT ON THE VOLLEYBALL COURT IN FULL SWEATS EVERY DAY AT 9:00! TO MAKE TIME, I'M CANCELLING DR. NORTH'S IMMUNOLOGY COURSE!

DUUUKE! DUUUKE!

SO LET'S GET OUT THERE AND... AND...

LOOK AT THAT. THEY'RE DOING THE WAVE.

THEY LOVE YOU, SIR!

ROBERT VESCO, AS AN INNOVATIVE FINANCIER OF THE HIGHEST ORDER, YOU HAVE MADE THE CARIBBEAN YOUR OYSTER, EARNING THE RESPECT OF LAW ENFORCEMENT OFFICERS EVERYWHERE.

WHEN YOUR OWN COUNTRY TURNED ITS BACK ON YOU, YOU SKILLFULLY MOVED YOUR ASSETS TO THE BAHAMAS WHERE YOU NOW OPERATE YOUR EMPIRE FROM AN UNDISCLOSED LOCATION.

IN PRIDEFUL RECOGNITION OF ALL YOU'VE GOTTEN AWAY WITH, THE BABY DOC COLLEGE OF PHYSICIANS TAKES GREAT PLEASURE IN CONFERRING ON YOU THE DEGREE OF DOCTOR OF ARTS AND LEISURE!

THANK YOU, PRESIDENT DUKE. I'M VERY PROUD THAT YOU...

OUR PLEASURE. LISTEN, BOBBY, WE NEED A GYM.

1985~1989

"I read *Doonesbury* every day. What else do you want to know?"

—Sal Consiglio, owner of Sally's Pizza, often mentioned in the strip

Admonished Quincy Jones, *"Check your egos at the door."*

Public criticism of Senator Jake Garn's "ultimate junket" aboard the space shuttle is led by *Doonesbury*, which dubs him "Barfin' Jake" (later shortened to "B.J." by his fellow astronauts).

Among Garn's chores in space: playing with 10 children's toys.

Trudeau's syndicate
convinces him to withdraw
"Silent Scream: The
Prequel," a week of strips
satirizing an anti-abortion
film. *The New Republic*
magazine runs all six
cartoons in its
June 10 issue.

AS THE MOMENT APPROACHES, TIMMY SEEMS ALMOST OBLIVIOUS TO THE CHARGED DEBATE THAT ATTENDS HIS FATE.

MINUTES LATER, THE DIE IS CAST. THE MOTHER HAS MADE THE UNCONSCIONABLE DECISION THAT SETS IN MOTION THE DOCTOR'S GRISLY PROCEDURE.

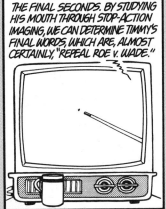

THE FINAL SECONDS. BY STUDYING HIS MOUTH THROUGH STOP-ACTION IMAGING, WE CAN DETERMINE TIMMY'S FINAL WORDS, WHICH ARE, ALMOST CERTAINLY, "REPEAL ROE v. WADE."

COMING UP: TIMMY REMEMBERED.

"HIS LOVE OF COUNTRY, HIS GENEROSITY FOR THOSE LESS FORTUNATE, HIS DISTINCTIVE ART..

..AND HIS WINNING AND COMPASSIONATE PERSONA MAKE HIM ONE OF OUR MOST REMARKABLE AND DISTINGUISHED AMERICANS..

..AND ONE WHO TRULY DID IT HIS WAY."
— Ronald Reagan
May 23, 1985

MEDAL OF FREEDOM RECIPIENT FRANK SINATRA DOING IT HIS WAY WITH TOMMY "FATSO" MARSON, DON CARLO GAMBINO, RICHARD "NERVES" FUSCO, JIMMY "THE WEASEL" FRATIANNO, JOSEPH GAMBINO AND GREG DEPALMA.

"HE HAS CARRIED ON HIS CRAFT WITH DISTINCTION AND HIGH PROFESSIONALISM..

HE HAS APPLIED HIS TALENTS TO THE BENEFIT OF MANKIND..

..AND TO THE UPLIFTING OF THE HUMAN SPIRIT."
— Citation for honorary degree, Stevens Institute, May 23, 1985

DR. FRANCIS SINATRA UPLIFTING THE SPIRITS OF ALLEGED HUMAN ANIELLO DELLACROCE, LATER CHARGED WITH THE MURDER OF GAMBINO FAMILY MEMBER CHARLEY CALISE.

June 13 **1985**

Numerous newspapers drop a series critical of Reagan's presentation of the Medal of Freedom to Frank Sinatra. The following week, Trudeau is denounced by a New Jersey congressman on the floor of the U.S. House of Representatives.

> " *He's as funny as a tumor.* "

—FRANK SINATRA
from the stage at Carnegie Hall

Q .... Did Sinatra ever sue?

A .... No, but his lawyer weighed in. He sent my employers a letter saying that I had completely misrepresented Mr. Sinatra's actions on such and such a day. Our position was that of *course* my portrayal of the incident was inaccurate—I'd made it up. We never heard from him again.

October 1 **1985**

A Florida State legislator introduces the so-called *"Doonesbury* Bill," which challenges a Palm Beach law requiring servants to carry ID cards. The president of the Florida Senate notes, "What I know about the ordinance is what I read in *Doonesbury.*" The bill passes nine months later.

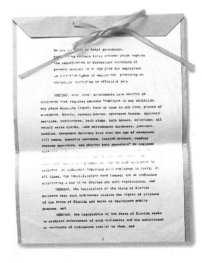

"Freedom's freedom," said the bill's sponsor, "You can't put a card-carrying thing in it. Let the commies do that."

BAA, SIR! BAA!

Trudeau, Charles Schulz, and Milt Caniff organize 175 syndicated cartoonists to focus attention on world hunger by devoting their Thanksgiving Day strips to the subject.

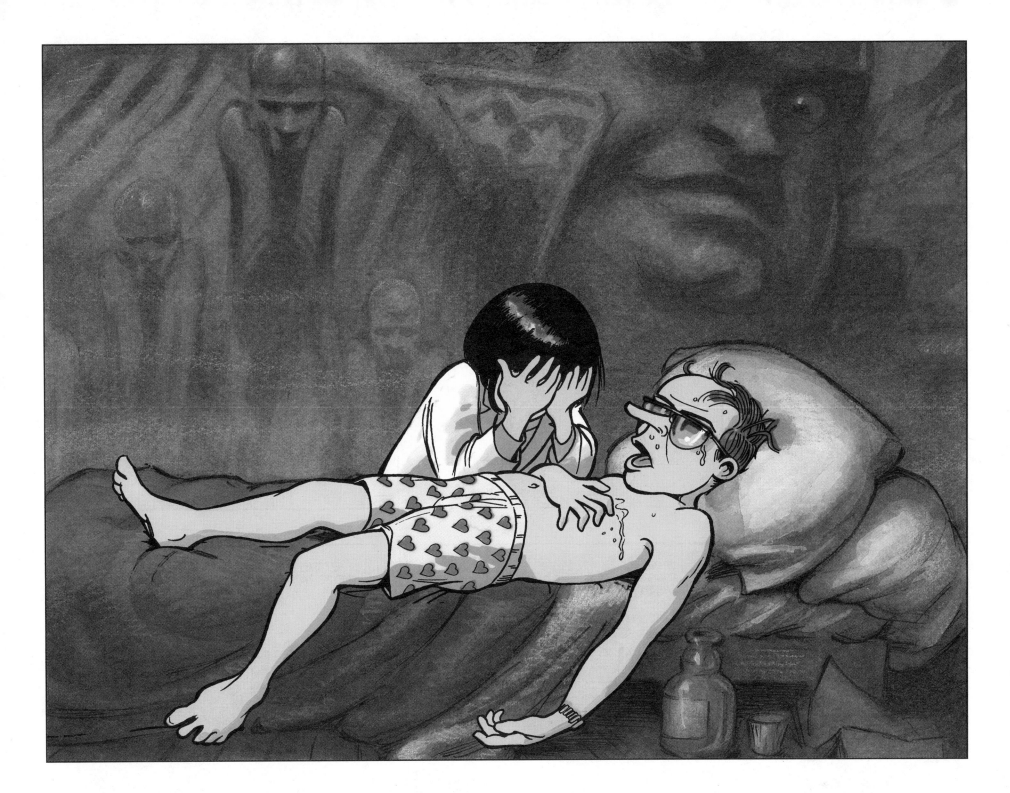

GEE, MISTER, DID YOU REALLY USED TO LIVE IN A COMMUNE?

Walden Commune 1972-1985

I SURE DID, YOUNGSTER.

GOSH! WHAT WAS IT LIKE?

Walden Commune 1972-1985

WHAT WAS IT LIKE? WELL, THAT'S A LONG STORY, SON. THINGS WERE VERY DIFFERENT BACK THEN.

Walden Commune 1972-1985

"TO BEGIN WITH, IT WAS AN AGE OF INNOCENCE.."

OKAY, SAY PAUL IS DEAD..

OH, WOW, I SEE WHAT YOU MEAN!

HEY, EVER LOOKED AT YOUR HANDS? LIKE, REALLY LOOKED AT YOUR HANDS?

"WHAT WAS WALDEN? WELL, SON, IT WAS ABOUT SHARING.."

GO AHEAD, THEY'RE YOURS! I KNOW YOU LOVE THESE BELLBOTTOMS, MIKE!

"..IT WAS ABOUT PERSONAL GROWTH.."

I..I THINK I'M READY TO GET IN TOUCH WITH MY FEMININE SIDE.

OH, B.D., I KNEW YOU'D COME AROUND!

"..AND PRINCIPLED ACTIVISM."

WORKED OUT A SLOGAN YET, MIKE?

NOT YET. IT'S HARD TO RE-PUDIATE INTERVEN-TIONISM WITHOUT SEEMING TO CHAM-PION OPPOSING VALUES.

OF COURSE, IT WASN'T ALL MORAL GLAMOUR..

ZZZZ!

Walden Commune 1972-1985

"WALDEN'S INFLUENCE RANGED FAR AND WIDE.."

DAD, CAN I EXPERIMENT WITH ALTERNATIVE LIFESTYLES LIKE MY IDOL ZONKER HARRIS?!

"..BUT ITS DENIZENS REMAINED UNAFFECTED.."

IT'S "TIME" MAGAZINE AGAIN.

ASK IF I CAN CALL BACK AFTER MY TURN DOING THE DISHES.

"..PREFERRING TO CULTIVATE THAT SIM-PLICITY AND NON-ACQUISITIVENESS THAT BECAME THEIR HALLMARK."

WE'RE RICH MEN, MICHAEL.

AMEN TO THAT, BRO!

YOUR CAR IS READY, SIR.

BE RIGHT THERE. OKAY, LAD, WHAT HAVE WE LEARNED TODAY?

NEVER TO ASK WHAT A COMMUNE WAS LIKE.

—CLINT EASTWOOD
commenting on Doonesbury *strips*

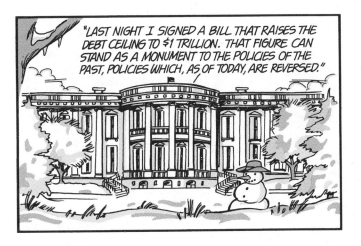

"Say it ain't so, Trudeau!" pleads the headline of a Wisconsin paper. Uncle Duke, discovered one morning "looking more inert than usual," is pronounced dead. *The St. Petersburg Times* runs a full obituary, as the *Paterson* (N.J.) *News* laments, "Duke was the kind of swine you couldn't help but like." The bizarre tragedy is ultimately softened by the revelation that Duke was not dead, but merely zombified and sold into slavery.

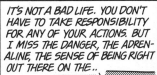

April 14 **1986**

Mark Slackmeyer broadcasts "Sleaze on Parade," the definitive list of Reaganite "back-scratchers, till-dippers, and conscience-cutters." Numerous papers drop the strip, among them *The Los Angeles Times*.

May 9 **1986**

The "Save the Gown" campaign urges readers to help "stabilize" Nancy Reagan's sagging inaugural gown. The Smithsonian sets up a special phone number to handle contributions and responses. Writes one Beverly Hills businessman, "Do something before it's too late."

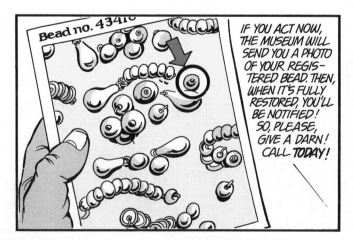

Doonesbury tour of "Contra Country" tracks the freedom fighters in Miami. Miffed Contra leader Arturo Cruz calls it "amusing satire," but says he prefers *Hagar the Horrible.*

205

March 25 1986

Doonesbury satirizes a Reagan speech by pinpointing Harlingen, Texas, as the likely target for a Sandinistan invasion. Sheriff Alex Perez requests riot gear, vowing, "If we don't get it, I guess we'll have to fight with tree limbs." The Harlingen Chamber of Commerce votes to spend $22,898 for a tourism ad campaign based on strips about the town.

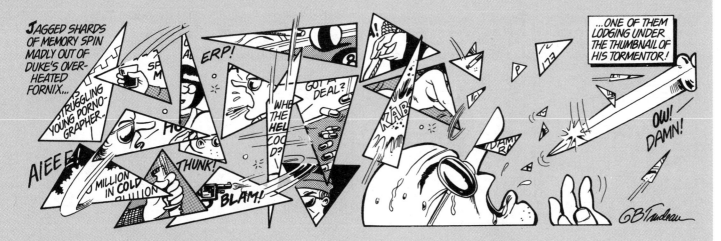

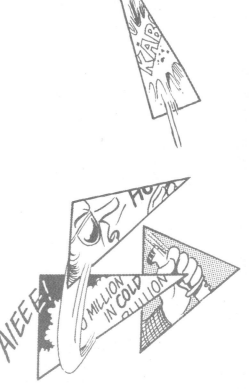

...AND I THINK IF WE CAN GET SOME CANVASSERS DOWN TO THE 5TH WARD...

SWEETEST! EXTRAORDINARY NEWS!

A BACHMAN'S WARBLER HAS BEEN SPOTTED OUT AT YOSEMITE! THROW ON A WRAP! I'VE GOT THE STUDEBAKER WARMED UP AND READY TO GO!

UM... I'M AFRAID I CAN'T GO OUT BIRD-WATCHING WITH YOU TODAY, DICK.

EGADS! WHY NOT?

I'M RUNNING FOR CONGRESS, DEAR.

I GUESS YOU DIDN'T HEAR ME. I SAID, A BACHMAN'S WARBLER!

YOU MUSTN'T FAIL, OLD BOY! A DOCUMENTED SIGHTING OF A BACHMAN'S WARBLER IS UNHEARD OF!

THE GARBO OF BIRDS! WHAT A FEATHER IN YOUR CAP IF... GOOD LORD! THERE IT IS! THERE IT... UNH!

WHA... WHAT HAPPENED? MY HEART IS... NO! GOD, NO! NOT NOW! NOT NOW, GOD!

GOD! I'LL MAKE YOU A DEA...

CHIRP!

FLUMP!

...AND TO ALL OF YOU WHO WORKED SO HARD FOR THIS VICTORY, MY GREAT THANKS! YOU'RE ALL ABSOLUTE DEARS!

KUDOS, TOO, TO MY TRUSTY CAMPAIGN MANAGER, JOANIE, AS WELL AS TO THE LOVE OF MY LIFE, HUSBAND DICK!

HE COULDN'T BE HERE TODAY, BUT I KNOW THAT THIS IS AS JOYOUS A DAY FOR HIM AS IT IS FOR ME!

WELL, GREAT. A MASSIVE CORONARY.

January 5 **1987**

Readers "clip 'n' save" pieces of "the Iranscam puzzle," hoping Trudeau will complete it. He doesn't. Numerous frustrated readers write in for "the missing piece." One woman speculates: "I think my cat ate it."

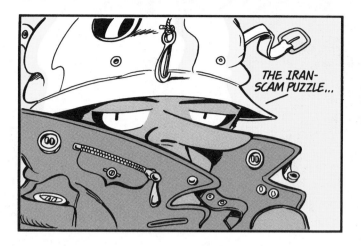

B.D., THIS IS SUCH AN HONOR TO BE ASKED TO JOIN THE STATE TASK FORCE ON SELF-ESTEEM!

I MEAN, THERE ARE **SO** MANY FILM ACTRESSES WITH MUCH MORE EXPERIENCE IN PERSONAL GROWTH!

WHAT A HIGH! I'VE NEVER FELT SUCH... SUCH **ELATION!** B.D., I THINK I'M ABOUT TO HAVE AN OUT-OF-BODY EXPERIENCE!

SURE YOU ARE, BOOPSIE.

BOOPSIE?... **BOOPSIE!**

I'M OVER HERE. IN THE BLENDER.

I'D LIKE TO CALL TO ORDER THIS FIRST MEETING OF THE CALIFORNIA TASK FORCE TO PROMOTE SELF-ESTEEM AND PERSONAL AND SOCIAL RESPONSIBILITY!

AS YOU KNOW, OUR MANDATE IS NOTHING LESS THAN TO STUDY THE RELATIONSHIP BETWEEN SELF-ESTEEM AND SOCIAL PROBLEMS, AND TO IDENTIFY PROGRAMS THAT ADDRESS THAT RELATIONSHIP!

OKAY, BEFORE WE ROLL UP OUR SLEEVES, LET ME FIRST JUST ASK HOW EVERYONE HERE FEELS ABOUT HIMSELF TODAY.

GOOD.

GOOD.

GOOD. GOOD.

GOOD!

GOOD.

GOOD, GOOD.

...AND I'VE ALSO DONE EXTENSIVE RESEARCH ON CAUSES OF TEEN DELINQUENCY.

THANK YOU, DOCTOR. WELL, BARBARA ANN, THAT JUST LEAVES YOU!

HI, EVERYONE. I'M BARBARA ANN BOOPSTEIN. I'M AN ACTRESS, A SPIRITUAL VOYAGER, AND A CHANNELER WHO SPEAKS FOR A REALLY GOOD-LOOKING 21,355-YEAR-OLD WARRIOR NAMED HUNK-RA!

DOES THAT MEAN HE'S ON THE TASK FORCE, TOO?

UM... LET ME CHECK THE BYLAWS. I KNOW HE CAN'T VOTE.

February 16 **1987**

Boopsie channels "Hunk-Ra" and joins the "totally historic" California Self-Esteem Task Force, an entity many mistakenly assume Trudeau invented. Says Task Force creator John Vasconcellos, "Satire is the highest form of indirect compliment."

"We thought the *Doonesbury* gang was pulling our leg again. We stand chastened and humbled to confess that we could not imagine anything with such a horse's-fanny title could be anything but make-believe."

— *Editorial, Salem Statesman-Journal*

February 1987

Mike Doonesbury is assigned to write condom ads for television. Papers in Montana, Utah, and Texas pull the series.

Post-modern protection, to go.

EMPLOYEE-OF-THE-MONTH SAL DOONESBURY TALKS ABOUT "DR. WHOOPEE"...

THE JOB ISN'T REALLY ABOUT MARKET SHARE — IT'S ABOUT PEOPLE, AND SOLVING THEIR PROBLEMS...

LAST MONTH I GOT AN URGENT CALL FROM A LARGE SORORITY AT A WELL-KNOWN EASTERN COLLEGE. SPRING BREAK WAS 12 HOURS AWAY, AND THEY NEEDED PROTECTION.

"I QUICKLY ROUTED THE ORDER ONTO OUR PRIORITY SATELLITE LINE, INSTANTLY ALERTING THE HOME OFFICE IN FLAGSTAFF..."

"WITHIN MINUTES, THE ORDER WAS PROCESSED AND PACKED AND WINGING ITS WAY TO THE ANXIOUS SORORITY SISTERS..."

'EVENING, MISS!

DOCTOR WHOOPEE! YOU **MADE** IT!

"DR. WHOOPEE," WHERE **PEOPLE** ARE JOB ONE.

SERVICE WITH A SMILE, **NOT A SMIRK!**

March **1987**

Roland Hedley embarks upon a "Return to Reagan's Brain" to jar loose Iranscam memories. Once again, some editors pull the series.

MARCH 26— TODAY WE MAKE OUR FINAL ASSAULT ON THE FORNIX, REAGAN'S MEMORY VAULT.

THE APPROACH IS ARDUOUS. NEURAL PASSAGES ARE SHRUNKEN AND CALCIFIED FROM CHRONIC DISUSE.

SUDDENLY... LIVE SYNAPSE!

CRAK!

WE LOSE A PORTER.

POOR DEVIL... HE KNEW THE RISKS. PUSH ON, LADS!

GOOD MORNING, SIR. HERE'S THAT LIST OF PHOTO OPS FOR YOU TO CHOOSE FROM.

OH, GOOD...

WHAT?

KEEP IN MIND WE'RE TRYING TO LIMIT PRESS ACCESS, SIR.

YOU MEAN, KEEP IT IN MIND WHILE I'M CHOOSING?

WHEN?

UH... YES, SIR.

WELL, OKAY, IF YOU SAY SO...

WHO?

ZIT! BZZT!

NO! NOO! NOT TWO THOUGHTS AT THE SAME TIME!

FWITZ!

CRAK!

APRIL 2, 1987 — BREAKTHROUGH! A ROUTINE CORE SAMPLE TAPS INTO A VEIN OF HIDDEN MEMORY!

GOOD GOD... IT EXISTS!

YES, BURIED BENEATH THE STRATA OF CONSCIOUS THOUGHT IS A MOTHERLODE OF SUPPRESSED MEMORIES. I AM SUDDENLY FACED WITH A MONSTROUS DILEMMA!

DO I BRING THIS IMPACTED INFORMATION TO THE SURFACE WHERE THE PRESIDENT CAN ACCESS IT? IS IT PROPER FOR A JOURNALIST TO PLAY SUCH A ROLE?

I AGONIZE OVER IT FOR DAYS.

WHAT WOULD BARBARA WALTERS DO?

" *Cartoonists occupy a special place in my heart. I hope that Garry Trudeau will remember that. It's heart. Not brain, heart.* **"**

—RONALD REAGAN

215

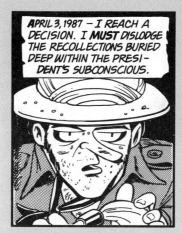

APRIL 3, 1987 – I REACH A DECISION. I **MUST** DISLODGE THE RECOLLECTIONS BURIED DEEP WITHIN THE PRESIDENT'S SUBCONSCIOUS.

FASHIONING A CRUDE INCENDIARY DEVICE FROM A BRANDY BOTTLE, I LET FLY.

KA-WHAM!

A RUSH OF MEMORY, SIR? ABOUT WHAT? I FORGET.

MR. & MRS. SHE-MOMMY

WHA... WHO... >GASP!< WHO ARE YOU?

MEDEVAC, MR. HEDLEY. JUST TAKE IT EASY. WE'RE GETTING YOU OUT OF HERE.

YOU'RE A LUCKY MAN. WE SPOTTED THE SMOKE IN THE CORTEX. OKAY! PULL HIM UP!

THAT WAS QUITE SOME STUNT YOU PULLED, PAL. IT RELEASED A FLOOD OF MEMORIES FOR THE PRESIDENT.

THE... THE MISSING PIECES?

AFRAID NOT. MOSTLY BASEBALL SCORES FROM THE '30s.

HOWARD, I DON'T KNOW ABOUT THIS...

TRUST ME, SIR. IT'S A PAINLESS WAY TO INCREASE YOUR ACCESSIBILITY – AND YOUR Q RATING!

R.R.

READY TO GO, MR. BAKER. THE PRESIDENT'S TEMPLATE IS LOADED ON DISC DRIVE.

FINE. START REPLICATION.

R.R.

BUT HOWARD...

STAND BY!

R.H.

GRE-GRE-GRE-GREETINGS! **RON HEADREST** HERE!

RON HEADREST TEST RUN, TEST RUN! DO RUN, RON! OPEN FIRE, M-M-MAKE THAT FILE, OPEN FILE!

HI, THIS IS YOUR H-H-HEAD OF STATE, HEAD OF STATE LOGGING IN!

SURE, WE'VE GOT PROBLEMS, BUT LET'S NOT THROW THE B-B-BABY OUT WITH THE DISHES!

GEE, I DON'T KNOW, HOWARD...

IT'S JUST TELEVISION, SIR. NO ONE WILL KNOW THE DIFFERENCE.

SO HOW DOES HART SOLVE HIS ALOOFNESS P-P-PROBLEM? BY DECLARING AT 11,000 FEET!

I SHOULD TALK! SO I DO! DO! I'M ALL HEART! FROM MY HEAD DOWN TO MY... MY... HEY! WHERE'S THE REST OF ME?

HELP ME OUT! I C-C-CAN'T DO THIS BY OURSELVES! YO! HOME BOY! ANY QUES-TIONS?

YES. AM I BEING BILLED FOR YOU?

NO! I'M NOT AVAILABLE IN YOUR AREA YET! YET!

NOW, NOW, T-T-TAKE JOE BIDEN! HE'S 45, BUT LIKE HART, 50, HE SWEARS HE'S A B-B-BABY BOOMER! ARE THESE GUYS PUSHY OR WHAT? OR WHAT? HOLD IT, BETTER COOL OFF...

I DON'T WANNA SAY MY HOME BASE CIRCUITRY IS H-H-HOT, BUT I JUST GOT PROPOSITIONED BY A LINEAR PHASE CERAMIC MICROFILTER!

THAT RE-RE-REMINDS ME! KIDS! NEED ROCK-SOLID INFORMATION ON SAFE SEX? CALL THIS NUMBER ON YOUR SCREEN!

(202) 456-1414

THAT DOES IT.

RING! RING! RING! RING! RING! BBRING! RING! RING! RING! RING! RING! RING! RING! RING! RING! RING!

Callers jam White House switchboards after Ron Headrest provides readers with the number to call for "rock-solid information on safe sex." Later in the day the White House takes revenge: White House spokesman Marlin Fitzwater orders the callers be given the number of Trudeau's employer.

Said a puzzled Fitzwater, "I wonder why he did that? Mischief, I guess."

217

"**Garry Trudeau** was shooting for a 'harmonic convergence' in today's *Doonesbury* cartoon, but city officials think he hit a 'discordant divergence' in his attempt to depict Palm Springs as a focal point for the experience. 'Nobody here did any harmonic converging,' said Mayor Frank Bogert. 'They all went up to Joshua Tree. He missed his geography.'"

—*Palm Springs Desert Sun,*
August 19, 1987

Panel 1: HARMONIC CONVERGENCE: MANKIND'S SECOND CHANCE.

Panel 2: IT IS WRIT LARGE, SOMEWHERE: "IN THE CUSP OF CONVERGING AGES, ONE BLINDING, HOLY MOMENT OF TRANSCENDENCE...

Panel 3: ...SHALL TRANSFORM THE ZEITGEIST WITH PERFECT SYNCHRONICITY, INTO THE PURE, INEFFABLE EXPRESSION OF INDIVISIBLE...

Panel 4: ...ONENESS." OH, RIGHT! YOU WERE EXPECTING ARTWORK OF *THAT*? SOME SORT OF SUNSET MIGHT'VE BEEN NICE.

Panel 5: HUNH... MUST HAVE DOZED OFF...

Panel 6: B.D.?... DID... DID IT HAPPEN? THREE GUESSES.

Panel 7: WHO... WHO AM I? AM I MY DIVINE SELF? OR STILL BOOPSIE? I FEEL LIKE..., LIKE... LIKE WHAT?

Panel 8: LIKE SHOPPING! YOU'RE STILL BOOPSIE.

Panel 9: NOTHING! *NADA!* SOME HARMONIC CONVERGENCE!

Panel 10: NO DISORIENTATION! NO DEJA VU! NO INVITATIONS TO JOIN A FEDERATION OF EXTRATERRESTRIALS! A TOTAL *BUST!*

Panel 11: BOOPSIE, I TRIED TO TELL YOU. SOMEWHERE IN THE WORLD PEOPLE MAY BE GETTING IT ON WITH THEIR DIVINE SPARKS...

Panel 12: ...BUT *NOT* IN PALM SPRINGS! I CAN'T UNDERSTAND IT. IT'S ON THE LIST OF SACRED ZIP CODES!

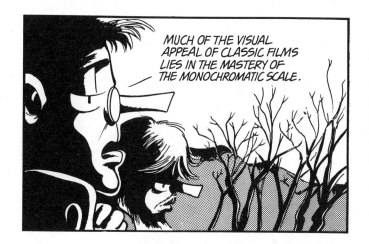

USA TODAY'S WASHINGTON AND THE WORLD MARKET SCOREBOARD

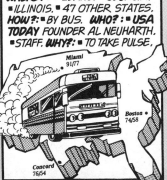

FOCUSING ON FUTURE BUSCAPADES: DON'T COUNT THEM OUT

221

WELL, I GUESS I CAN'T PUT IT OFF ANY LONGER...

YEAH. THIS IS RICK REDFERN FROM THE "CHARACTER" DESK. I'D LIKE THOSE FILES ON GARY HART'S PRIVATE LIFE SENT BACK UP, PLEASE.

UH... BY WHEN?

BACK IN THE THICK OF IT, I SEE!

IF YOU'RE HERE TO TAUNT ME, CARL, YOU'LL HAVE TO TAKE A NUMBER.

NO, NO, JUST WONDERED HOW YOU WERE BEARING UP.

NOT WELL. NAILING DOWN GARY HART'S CHARACTER DEFECTS IS NOT EXACTLY UPLIFTING WORK.

WELL, RICK, LOOK AT IT THIS WAY. IF YOU DON'T DO IT, SOMEONE FAR LESS SUITED TO IT WILL!

CHARACTER PATROL! PULL OVER, SENATOR!

SENATOR HART! IS IT TRUE YOU DIDN'T REALLY LEARN ANY LESSONS FROM THE DONNA RICE AFFAIR?

I DON'T THINK THE PUBLIC IS INTERESTED IN THE ANSWER TO THAT QUESTION, ROLAND...

THE PUBLIC IS INTERESTED IN SUBSTANCE! PEOPLE ARE HUNGRY TO HEAR ABOUT ISSUES, ISSUES LIKE... STRATEGIC INVESTMENT MATRICES!

STAND BACK! HE'S USING THE POWER OF IDEAS!

ENLIGHTENED REVITALIZATION! PROGRESSIVE ENGAGEMENT!

December 3 **1987**

Defending Larry Flynt's satire of Jerry Falwell before the Supreme Court, attorney Alan Isaacman argues that the parody is entitled to the same First Amendment protection as *Doonesbury* spoofs of George Bush.

The Prince of Inner Space.

WE'RE DOWN ON THE STREET NOW TALKING TO INDUSTRIALIST **BIG JIM ANDREWS!** ANY REACTION TO YOUR COLD WAR BLOWOUT, JIM?

HOW SWEET IT IS, ROLAND, HOW **SWEET** IT IS!

THE REDS GAVE US A REAL RUN FOR OUR MONEY, I'LL TELL YOU THAT! BUT WE BEAT THEM WITH THE BASICS: HARD CURRENCY, CHEAP WHEAT AND GOOD ROCK 'N' ROLL!

JIM'S WIFE, KATHY, IS ALSO WITH US! ANY REACTION, KATHY?

I'M JUST GLAD IT'S OVER. JIM'S BEEN A COLD WARRIOR FOR OVER 35 YEARS.

WELL, WEL-COME HOME, SOLDIER! WHERE YOU HEADED?

THE SUB-URBS!

WE'RE GO-ING TO CEL-EBRATE OUR WAY OF LIFE! JUST THE TWO OF US!

AS THE PANDEMONIUM CONTINUES IN TIMES SQUARE, I'M NOW TALKING TO FREE MARKETEER PHIL SLACKMEYER! PHIL, IT'S A GREAT DAY FOR WALL STREET TODAY, ISN'T IT?

YES, IT IS, AND YOU KNOW, ROLAND, IT'S ABOUT TIME! WALL STREET HAS GOTTEN RAPPED A LOT LATELY, BUT IT WAS THERE THAT THE BATTLE AGAINST THE STATE-PLANNED ECONOMY WAS WON!

SURE, SOMETIMES THE COLD WAR GOT DIRTY. SOMETIMES WE HAD TO CUT A FEW CORNERS TO MAINTAIN CASH FLOW. BUT I'D DO IT ALL OVER AGAIN, EVEN IF IT MEANT DOING MORE TIME!

HEY, THAT'S RIGHT. WHAT ARE YOU DO-ING OUT OF...

AMNESTY.

YOU KNOW, BOOPSIE, WE CAN TALK ABOUT THE AFGHAN REBS, WE CAN TALK ABOUT SOLIDARITY, BUT I GATHER YOU FEEL THE **REAL** COLD WAR SHOCK TROOPS HAVE BEEN WESTERN ROCKERS, RIGHT?

THAT'S RIGHT, ROLAND! ONCE YOU HAVE A BILLY JOEL IN THE U.S.S.R., OR A GEORGE MICHAEL IN CHINA, THERE'S JUST **NO** TURNING BACK! AS THEY SAY, "ROCK'N'ROLL WILL SET YOU FREE!"

ROCK 'N' ROLL IS ALL **ABOUT** CHALLENGES TO AUTHORITY. SO INSTEAD OF B-1's, WE SHOULD BE SENDING THEM U-2! BEFORE USING STINGERS, WE SHOULD HIT THEM WITH **STING!**

LET'S MAKE 'EM BOP 'TIL THEY **DROP!** LET'S...

EXCUSE ME, BOOPSIE! HERE COME THE MERRILL LYNCH **PRANC-ING BULLS!**

GORE, THE DEMOCRATIC CANDIDATE, WAS BORN ALBERT, PRINCE OF THE TENNESSEE VALLEY...

I CAN'T SEEM TO SHAKE THIS FEELING OF... OF... DESTINY!

SON OF ALBERT THE ELDER, THE YOUNG PRINCE GREW UP IN THE SHADOW OF THE CAPITOL DOME.

HEY! DOME! YOU'RE BLOCKING MY LIGHT!

HE ONCE SAT ON THE LAP OF VICE PRESIDENT RICHARD NIXON.

WHAT A THRILL!

IT WAS AN UNUSUAL CHILDHOOD.

COULD YOU PASS THE KETCHUP, PLEASE, MR. SECRETARY?

@B Trudeau

ALONE AMONG THE DEMOCRATIC CONTENDERS, TENNESSEE'S PRINCE ALBERT HAD BEEN PREPARED FOR POWER FROM BIRTH.

ENOUGH PREPARATION! I'M READY!

HE CERTAINLY **SEEMED** READY. DEPENDING ON HIS AUDIENCE, THE HARVARD-TRAINED PRINCE WAS, BY TURNS, WELL-VERSED...

KEATS PUT IT BEST.

...WELL-PREPARED...

MY POSITION ON BOOSTER PHASE BATTLE MANAGEMENT TECHNOLOGIES HAS EVOLVED.

...AND BILINGUAL.

Y'ALL WANNA HEAR MAH COON DAWG CALL?

@B Trudeau

OTHER PEOPLE WERE RUNNING FOR PRESIDENT, BUT THIS DIDN'T FAZE PRINCE ALBERT...

OTHER PEOPLE SHOULDN'T BE PRESIDENT. **I** SHOULD.

AL GORE

... SO HE WENT TO IOWA...

IOWA IS KEY!

...WHERE HIS SUPPORT WAS TOO LOW TO BE MEASURED.

0% AND FALLING!

IOWA IS A JOKE!

@B Trudeau

THE PRINCE ISSUED A SHERMANESQUE STATEMENT.

I WILL TAKE THE SOUTH!

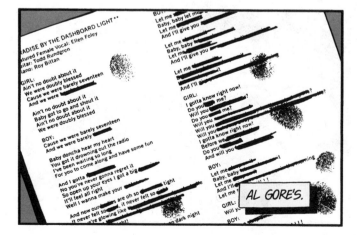

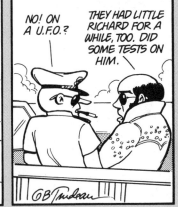

LOOK, DOLE OR KEMP PROBABLY WOULD HELP THE TICKET, BUT THEY BOTH COME ON TOO STRONG FOR GEORGE.

WHO, THEN?

I DON'T KNOW. BUT THE CHOICE HAS TO BE A BOLD ONE. WE'VE GOT TO DO SOMETHING TO TURN THE POLLS AROUND.

IN THE FINAL ANALYSIS, WE NEED SOMEONE WHO CAN ADD SOME HEFT, SOME BEEF, SOME *WEIGHT* TO THE TICKET!

HI, GUYS! ANYONE FOR GOLF?

NOT NOW, DANNY...

HOW ABOUT PEE-WEE HERMAN?

YOU SURE NOBODY WANTS TO PLAY GOLF?

WE'RE KIND OF BUSY HERE, DANNY... HEY... DANNY!

WHAT ABOUT DANNY, SIR? *HE* SURE AS HECK WOULDN'T OVER-SHADOW YOU!

UH... YOU SURE?

WHAT'S GOING ON HERE?

WE'RE PICKING A RUNNING MATE, DAN. GO OVER AND STAND NEXT TO THE VICE PRESIDENT, WOULD YOU?

WOW... EXCITEMENT CITY!

I LIKE HIM, I *LIKE* HIM!

A POLL WAS QUICKLY TAKEN.

MA'AM, WOULD YOU VOTE FOR A CANDIDATE IF HE BORE A FAINT RESEMBLANCE TO ROBERT REDFORD?

ARE YOU NUTS? OF *COURSE*, I WOULD!

SURE, I'D VOTE FOR HIM. ANYONE THAT GOOD LOOKING MUST STAND FOR REALLY GOOD THINGS.

HE'D SURE HAVE MY VOTE.

YES, IT'S TIME FOR A CHANGE. I THINK MOST WOMEN WANT A REALLY HOT GUY TO BE IN CHARGE OF THE COUNTRY.

THE POLL, ALAS, WAS NOT ADJUSTED FOR SARCASM.

THEY WANT SOMEONE CUTE!

YOU GOT THE JOB, DANO!

OH BOY, OH BOY!

233

Q ···· Was the Bush stuff personal?

A ···· Of course not. It's never personal. At the risk of sounding like Sonny Corleone, it's my job. The Bushes never got that. Jeb Bush once drew me aside at the Republican Convention and said he had only two words for me: "Walk softly." Now, telling a cartoonist to walk softly is like asking a professional wrestler to show a little class. It's just not a productive suggestion. I went home and redoubled my efforts.

MR. BUSH, CAN YOU DISCERN ANY REAL MANDATE IN YOUR VICTORY YESTERDAY?

ABSO-LUTELY!

I HAVE A MANDATE TO SAY THE PLEDGE OF ALLEGIANCE, TO NOT JOIN THE ACLU, TO NOT PERMIT MURDERERS OUT ON WEEKEND FURLOUGHS!

I THINK WHAT THE AMERICAN PEOPLE TOLD US IN NO UN-CERTAIN TERMS YESTERDAY IS THAT THEY WANT SOME-ONE WHO IS **NOT** MICHAEL DUKAKIS!

AND YOU ARE THAT MAN?

IT GETS BACK TO EXPERIENCE. I'VE SPENT A **LIFETIME** NOT BEING SOMEONE!

WHAT SORT OF MAN IS THE NEW PRESIDENT-ELECT? WE ASKED DISTINGUISHED THINK-TANKIST J.S. HAVEL...

WE STILL DON'T KNOW. FOR REASONS BEST GRASPED BY HIS HANDLERS, HE DECLINED TO PUT FORTH A POSITIVE PERSONA.

SINCE HIS CAMPAIGN WAS LARGE-LY DRIVEN BY NEGATIVE IMAGERY, PEOPLE ARE NOW UNABLE TO THINK OF HIM IN TERMS OTHER THAN WHAT HE IS **NOT**!

PRESIDENT-ELECT UN-DUKAKIS WAS NOT AVAILABLE FOR COMMENT.

NAKED AMBITION IS RARELY A PRETTY SIGHT. BUT IN THIS ELECTION'S VICTOR, IT BECAME A GROTESQUE SPECTACLE.

HERE WAS A MAN WHOM EVEN HIS ENEMIES AGREED WAS ONCE THE MODEL OF DECENCY, ENGAG-ING IN SYSTEMATIC SLANDER IN PURSUIT OF THE PRESIDENCY.

WILL THERE BE SOME TER-RIBLE PRICE TO PAY FOR HIS TRANSFORMATION? AS GEORGE HERBERT WALKER UN-DUKAKIS RETURNS TO HIS VICE PRESIDENTIAL DU-TIES TODAY, ONLY **HE** KNOWS FOR SURE!

GEORGIE! YOU HAVEN'T BEEN RE-TURNING MY CALLS, BABE!

HOW'D YOU GET IN HERE?

The *Winston-Salem Journal* drops a strip on the R.J. Reynolds Tobacco Co. because "it would be personally offensive to its employees." It is the first time the strip has been pulled in deference to a corporation.

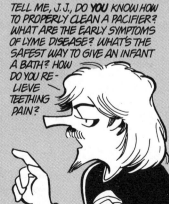

I CAN'T BELIEVE WE JUST LEFT LITTLE NO-NAME WITH ZONKER.

SHE'LL BE FINE.

WHAT IF HE JUST PLOPS HER IN FRONT OF THE TUBE AND ZONES OUT ALL DAY?

HE WON'T. HE TOLD ME HIMSELF HE DOESN'T BELIEVE IN UNSUPERVISED TELEVISION.

OKAY, NOW, THAT'S CALLED "CROSS-DRESSING." CAN YOU SAY "CROSS-DRESSING"?

TRY THE PEARLS, PHIL!

ZONKER?

MIKE!

HOW'D IT GO?

BETTER GET IN HERE! QUICK!

WHAT? THE BABY...?

THANK GOD YOU'RE HERE!

WHAT? WHAT'S WRONG?

UH...NOTHING. IT'S FIVE. I'M OFF DUTY.

NIGHTY, NIGHT, PUMPKIN!

OH, I ALMOST FORGOT TO TELL YOU...

TODAY SHE CALLED ME "MAMA"! ISN'T THAT WILD? SHE CALLED THE BABYSITTER "MAMA"!

ALWAYS A MOMENT EVERY MOTHER TREASURES, ZONK.

WELL, I THOUGHT SO, SO I VIDEOTAPED IT.

I'M BAD! I'M BAAD...

237

ROOTS.

GET **OUT** THERE, CHRISTIAN SCUM! THE LIONS ARE **HUNGRY**!

A SPLENDID ENTERTAINMENT, EH, FLAUVIUS IMPERVIOUS?

PERHAPS. BUT IT PANDERS TO SUCH BASE, MOB INSTINCTS.

DON'T BE SO CONDESCENDING, FLAUVIUS! THIS IS WHAT THE ROMAN PUBLIC WANTS! NO ONE IS FORCING THEM TO BE HERE!

SURE, BUT...

HAVE A PITY, MAN! THE EMPIRE IS CRUMBLING AROUND US! IF WATCHING A FEW MARTYRS GET TORN APART HELPS PEOPLE GET THEIR MINDS OFF THEIR PROBLEMS, THEN I'M **PROUD** TO BE PART OF IT!

BY JUPITER, YOU'RE RIGHT. I NEVER THOUGHT OF IT THAT WAY. BY OFFERING A PUBLIC DISTRACTION, YOU'RE SOFTENING THE ROUGH EDGES OF LIFE!

YOU'RE A GOOD MAN, GERALDO RIVERIBUS.

I TRY.

March 27 **1989**

A three-week series in which Congresswoman Lacey Davenport discovers that her aide Andy Lippincott is suffering from AIDS is widely discussed. A few papers drop the series, but many AIDS activists approve. Christian Heran, an AIDS sufferer in San Francisco, tells UPI, "The epidemic does have its funny side."

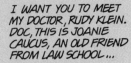

ANDY, I'M SORRY I FAINTED, I...

DON'T WORRY ABOUT IT, JOANIE. EVERYONE'S A LITTLE SHOOK UP WHEN THEY FIRST SEE ME. THANKS FOR COMING.

I WANT YOU TO MEET MY DOCTOR, RUDY KLEIN. DOC, THIS IS JOANIE CAUCUS, AN OLD FRIEND FROM LAW SCHOOL...

HELLO, DOCTOR.

DR. KLEIN'S BEEN CARING FOR AIDS PATIENTS FOR SEVEN YEARS. SO FAR HE'S GOT A PERFECT RECORD!

A PERFECT RECORD?

I'VE LOST THEM ALL.

BUT HE MAKES THE BEST MORPHINE COCKTAIL IN TOWN!

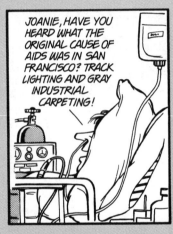

JOANIE, HAVE YOU HEARD WHAT THE ORIGINAL CAUSE OF AIDS WAS IN SAN FRANCISCO? TRACK LIGHTING AND GRAY INDUSTRIAL CARPETING!

HEE, HEE, HEE, HEE!

WHAT'S WRONG, TOO SUBTLE?

ANDY, HOW CAN YOU JOKE?

HOW CAN YOU NOT?

JOANIE, WHAT YOU HAVE TO UNDERSTAND IS THERE'S A LOT OF ANGER ON THIS WARD. FOR MOST PATIENTS, AIDS IS A STIGMA ON TOP OF A STIGMA. SOCIETY HAS YET TO COME TO TERMS WITH IT.

ANDY USES HUMOR TO SOFTEN THE RAGE HE FEELS AND TO HELP HIM FACE THE ABYSS. I ENCOURAGE IT, BECAUSE AIDS CARE IS ABOUT HELPING PEOPLE COPE, HELPING THEM DIE WITH DIGNITY...

EVERY DAY I GO IN TO SEE ANDY, AND HE MAKES SOME TERRIBLE JOKE ABOUT HIS LESIONS, AND I PLAY STRAIGHT MAN, AND WE'RE BOTH SCREAMING INSIDE, BUT IT'S BETTER THAN GOING MAD.

AND ON YOUR DAYS OFF?

I UNWIND. HOLD UP CONVENIENCE STORES. THAT SORT OF THING.

August 13 1989

700 people clip Mr. Butts' coupon promising free cigarettes ("recipient must be under-aged") and mail it to the Tobacco Institute. When asked what the response indicated, Institute spokeswoman Brennan Dawson notes, "I think it shows the kids read the comics."

Buttsie and Mr. Jay:
The gateway drugs kibitz in Mike's
compromised imagination.

HEY, **TEENS!** MR. **BUTTS** HERE! EVER WONDER WHY THERE'S SO MUCH PEER PRESSURE TO **SMOKE?**

IT'S BECAUSE YOUR FRIENDS DON'T WANT YOU TO **MISS OUT!** GETTING HOOKED ON CIGARETTES IS **FUN** —AND SURPRISINGLY EASY!

FOR JUST A FEW DOLLARS A DAY, YOU'LL HAVE A GLAMOROUS NEW HABIT FOR **LIFE!**

ME, NEXT! ME, NEXT!

Winston

IS IT **SAFE?** HECK, **YES!** JUST CHECK OUT THE **FILTER!**

BELIEVE ME, **NUTHIN'** GETS BY **THAT** BABY!

MR. BUTTS TALKS TO **TEEN-AGERS!**

: DON'T WORRY ABOUT CANCER, KIDS! YOU'RE TEEN-AGERS— YOU'RE **IMMORTAL!**

AND BELIEVE ME, THERE'S **NOTHING** COOLER THAN A 15-YEAR-OLD WALKING DOWN THE STREET WITH A CIGARETTE! HERE, TRY ONE!

CLIK!

GREAT TASTE, EH, JIMMY?

YEAH... >COUGH!< REALLY EXCEL- LENT... >HACK!< =HACK!<

DON'T WORRY, FOLKS — HE'LL GET THE **HANG** OF IT!

CHOKE! COUGH! COUGH! HACK!

THANX, MR. BUTTS!

...AND HE WORE WHITE GLOVES AND THIS BIG SMARMY GRIN!

MIKE, I THINK YOU READ TOO MANY "ZAP COMIX" AT COLLEGE...

NO, NO, THE DREAM **MEANS** SOMETHING! MY CONSCIENCE IS SENDING ME A VERY CLEAR SIGNAL!

I WON'T DO IT! I'M GOING TO TELL THE AGENCY I **WON'T** DO THE SMOKING CAMPAIGN!

HEE, HEE! DON'T WORRY, FOLKS! NO-BODY SEZ "NO" TO MR. BUTTS!

WINK! WINK!

WE'VE GOT A SPECIAL TREAT ON TAP FOR YOU, NIGHT OWLS! WITH ME RIGHT NOW IS VICE PRESIDENT **DAN QUAYLE**, WHO WAS RECENTLY NAMED "1989 FATHER OF THE YEAR" BY THE NATIONAL FATHER'S DAY COMMITTEE!

"1989 FATHER OF THE YEAR"! THAT'S QUITE AN HONOR, MR. VICE PRESIDENT!

YES, IT IS, MARK...

BUT, YOU KNOW, BASICALLY IT'S A TRIBUTE TO **MY** FATHER! HE'S THE ONE WHO SET THE EXAMPLE FOR ME IN THE PARENTING DEPARTMENT!

FOR INSTANCE, ONCE A WEEK, HE'D MAKE ME SIT DOWN AND RECITE **GOLDEN'S RULE**, WHICH GOES "DO WITH OTHERS WHAT THEY WOULD HAVE YOU UNDO..."

"...OR WHAT THEY THEMSELVES DO TO TRESPASS AGAINST THOSE WHO DO IT WHETHER OR NOT THEY...THEY...UM..."

WHATEVER. THE IMPORTANT THING WAS THAT YOU GUYS TALKED!

THAT'S RIGHT, MARK! WHICH IS WHY THE CHIP DIDN'T FALL VERY FAR FROM THE BLOCK!

"Give me your tired, your poor,
your Chinese undergraduates."

THAT'S YOUR NEW WIFE, JIM?

PRETTY EASY ON THE EYE, HUH? AND I'LL TELL YOU, SHE'S QUITE A LIVE WIRE!

SHE WORKS LIKE A DEMON AT THIS LITTLE DECORATING BUSINESS I SET UP FOR HER, AND YET SHE STILL PENCILS IN PLENTY OF TIME FOR ME! I CAN'T TELL YOU HOW SUPPORTIVE THIS LITTLE GAL IS!

KATHY WAS ALWAYS TEARING ME DOWN, REMINDING ME OF WHERE I CAME FROM. I JUST WASN'T GETTING MUCH RETURN ON MY 25-YEAR INVESTMENT!

JIM, SHE RAISED YOUR KIDS.

NOT SO WELL, FRANKLY. I HAD TO SEND THEM BOTH TO MILITARY SCHOOL.

SHE'S HIS **WIFE**? SHE CAN'T BE **HALF** HIS AGE!

WELL, JIM SAYS IT'S LOVE...

RIGHT! THAT LITTLE OPPORTUNING...

IT'S NOT ABOUT MONEY, MARILOU, THEY SIGNED A PRENUPTIAL AGREEMENT.

I DON'T CARE! THE WOMAN BROKE UP A 25-YEAR MARRIAGE!

WE DON'T KNOW THAT, MARILOU. SHE MIGHT NOT HAVE BEEN INVOLVED!

©B Trudeau

HOW ARE THE KIDS TAKING IT?

JUST FINE. ONE OF THEM USED TO DATE HER.

IT'S NOT FOR ME, OF COURSE, BUT A YOUNG NEW WIFE **DOES** GIVE JIM A DYNAMIC IMAGE. A WOMAN LIKE THAT **VALIDATES** HIS SUCCESS IN THE WORLD!

WELL, IF YOU ASK ME, THE ONLY THING IT VALIDATES IS HIS FAILURE AT HOME.

©B Trudeau

DEAR, IF YOU NEED TO BE SEEN WITH A BIMBO, WHY DON'T YOU JUST RENT ONE FROM AN ESCORT SERVICE?

COULD I?

Q .... Any repercussions from the Teheran Critics Circle strips?

A .... Only a temporary security upgrade. That spring I attended the American Booksellers Association Convention, and the organizers insisted that any author who had taken a public position on the *fatwa* be accompanied by a bodyguard. I spent two days strolling around the booths, trying to make small talk with booksellers while my intense companion scrutinized the crowds for potential assassins.

The worst part of having a bodyguard is that you get used to it. When he finally put me in a car for the airport, I don't believe I ever felt more vulnerable in my life.

HI! RECOVERED PROBLEM TANNIST ZONKER HARRIS HERE!

IF YOU'RE LIKE ME, BY NOW YOU'VE KICKED YOUR DANGEROUS SUN HABIT. SO HOW DO YOU CONTINUE LEADING AN ACTIVE, OUTDOOR LIFE WITHOUT RUNNING THE RISK OF ACQUIRING AN UNSIGHTLY TAN?

EASY, NOW THAT THERE'S **NERD-CARE**™! **NERD-CARE**™ IS THE MEDICALLY PROVEN BLEACHING LOTION THAT 3 OUT OF 4 PROFESSIONAL COMPUTER PROGRAMMERS SAY THEY WOULD WANT WITH THEM IF THEY WERE STRANDED ON A DESERT ISLAND.

NERD-CARE™ RESTORES THE SKIN'S NATURAL PALENESS, GIVING YOU THAT HIP, HEALTHY PALLOR THAT SAYS YOU'RE A SERIOUS PERSON, THAT YOU HAVEN'T BEEN WASTING YOUR LIFE ON A BEACH!

SO GO AHEAD, LIGHTEN UP WITH **NERD-CARE**™ FOR THE FINEST IN PALE.

NOW AVAILABLE IN PALE, WHITER SHADE OF PALE, AND NEW, MINTY GREEN!

September 11 1989

Doonesbury sequence breaks true story of Barbara Bush's encounter with a rat in the White House swimming pool.

THE BUSH WHITE HOUSE, BY ALL ACCOUNTS, AN OPEN AND HOSPITABLE EXECUTIVE MANSION.

YET CORDIALITY HAS ITS LIMITS, AND ONE MORNING THEY ARE UNEXPECTEDLY TESTED...

...WHEN, DURING HER DAILY SWIM, THE FIRST LADY ENCOUNTERS A *MOST* UNWELCOME GUEST...

A RAT.

AIEE!

'MORNING, MRS. B! MIND IF I JOIN YOU?

A RAT IS ENCOUNTERED IN THE WHITE HOUSE SWIMMING POOL BY A STARTLED, BREAST-STROKING FIRST LADY...

EEK!

POOLSIDE, THE PRESIDENT IS IMMOBILIZED. APART FROM THE SHEER IMPROBABILITY OF VERMIN IN THE WHITE HOUSE...

...THE PRESENCE OF THE RAT REPRESENTS SOMETHING POPPY FEARS ABOVE ALL ELSE...

A DECISION.

SURE, I COULD GO SEMI-BALLISTIC HERE, BUT, HEY, WHY NOT LOOK AT **ALL** THE OPTIONS BEFORE...

GEORGE! *DO* SOMETHING!

...AND MY RECOMMENDATION WOULD BE TO NEUTRALIZE THE ANIMAL.

THANKS, GENERAL. ANY OTHER SUGGESTIONS?

SIR, THE IMPORTANT THING IS TO DISTANCE YOURSELF FROM THE RAT! REMEMBER THE TROUBLE THAT CARTER RAN INTO WITH THE ATTACK RABBIT!

GOOD POINT, JOHN. STILL, I'D LIKE MORE INPUT ON POSSIBLE COURSES OF ACTION. LET'S SET UP A STUDY GROUP TO OUTLINE THE OPTIONS!

EXCUSE ME, MR. PRESIDENT. THE RAT HAS CORNERED YOUR WIFE.

HANG ON, BARB! *GOSH*, SHE'S A GOOD SPORT!

1990~1995

"Vile and disgraceful attack!
Untruthful and scurrilous!"

—Rep. Dick Schulze on Doonesbury, speaking
from the floor of the U.S. House of Representatives

252

March 26 **1990**

Several papers drop *Doonesbury* series on Dan Quayle's purchase of an anatomically correct gag doll during an official visit to Chile. The Pine Bluff, Arkansas *Commercial* explained, "Those of us in the newspaper business are obliged to cover the tasteless, but we see no reason to publish material on this page that is both tasteless and boring."

Handcrafted in Chile: The anatomically explicit Dan Quayle doll.

AT HIS BOSS'S BIDDING, A SECRET SERVICE AGENT PRESSED A FEW DOLLARS INTO THE OLD SHOPKEEPER'S HAND...

...AND PEDRO, THE ANATOMICALLY EXPLICIT GAG DOLL WAS QUICKLY SPIRITED OUT OF TOWN...

...AND ONTO THE AWAITING AIR FORCE TWO...

UNITED STATES OF AM

...WHERE IT CONTINUED TO EMBARRASS EVERYONE.

DANNY! GET THAT OUT OF HERE!

HEE, HEE! WHAT A RIOT!

THWAT!

IT WAS AN ASTONISHING TURN OF EVENTS FOR PEDRO, THE ANATOMICALLY EXPLICIT GAG DOLL.

FOR 17 LONG YEARS, HE HAD SAT, IGNORED, ON A DUSTY SHELF IN A CHILEAN SOUVENIR STALL.

BUT NOW, AS AIR FORCE TWO TOUCHED DOWN ON U.S. SOIL, IT SEEMED THE LITTLE DOLL'S STORY WAS ABOUT TO END HAPPILY.

IN FACT, IT WAS JUST BEGINNING.

FOR ME? WHAT IS IT?

HEE, HEE! STAND BACK, SIR!

COME IN, BAR. I'LL BE THROUGH IN A MINUTE...

GEORGE?

...I'M JUST GOING OVER THE REPORTS ON DANNY'S TRIP TO SOUTH AMERICA.

HOW'D HE DO?

WELL, THERE WERE A FEW BUMPS. BUT NOTHING TOO SERIOUS.

GREAT! DID HE BRING YOU THIS CUTE LITTLE...

NO! DON'T...

SPROING!

Sunday strip features "protest stamps," which Zonker urges readers to affix to correspondence in opposition to proposed postal rate increase. United States Postal Service officials issue an internal alert bulletin. Postmaster General Anthony M. Frank calls the strip "a mistake."

"They're definitely illegal," said a spokesman. The fine: $300.

May 24 **1990**

Andy Lippincott finally succumbs to AIDS. *The San Francisco Chronicle* runs news of his death on its obituary page, and Andy is remembered by a square in NAMES Project AIDS Memorial Quilt.

Andy's square: Its author takes a few liberties.

In a 20th anniversary profile, Trudeau describes himself as "Joan of Arc's spouse."

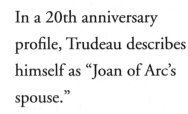

259

"Why was Garry

Trudeau, the creator of *Doonesbury*, bounced from a USO-sponsored trip to Saudi Arabia? The response from U.S. Headquarters in Riyadh: Trudeau wasn't barred; his visit was merely postponed 'due to logistics and transportation limitations.'

A senior administration official denied the White House knew anything of Trudeau's trip, but added: 'If we had known, we would have bumped him, too.'"

—*Newsweek,*
November 26, 1990

Sunshine warriors: Trudeau
smuggled in his proxies.

Full Metal Buttons: Commemorating the Build-up, 1990.

Q ···· You wrote about the Gulf War for almost 250 consecutive days. Overkill?

A ···· Possibly, but I was getting great feedback — and ideas — from military personnel in the field. When I finally got over there, the troops invited me aboard their Blackhawks and Bradleys and within a week had me driving a M-1A tank. They were too young — and I was too flushed — to remember Dukakis.

HEY, **YOUNGSTERS**! I'M NOT ALLOWED TO TELL WHERE I AM, BUT IF I COULD, WOULD YOU BE ABLE TO PLACE IT ON A MAP? FIND OUT WITH MY "KUWAITI KWIK KWIZ"! TEST YOUR MIDEAST I.Q. BY IDENTIFYING THE FOLLOWING PLAYERS ON THE G.I.'s HELMET: A-SAUDI ARABIA; B-EGYPT; C-IRAQ; D-IRAN; E-JORDAN; F-ISRAEL; G-SYRIA; I-OMAN; J-YEMEN; K-LIBYA; L-QATAR, M-TURKEY; N-KUWAIT; O-LEBANON! CORRECT ANSWERS ARE PRINTED TO THE RIGHT! GOOD LUCK!

SPECIAL NOTE TO PARENTS AND TEACHERS:

WARNING: DUE TO THE VOLATILE NATURE OF THE MIDEAST CRISIS, SOME OF THE EXISTING BORDERS MAY BE DATED BY THE TIME OF PUBLICATION. THE ANSWERS INDICATED REPRESENT OUR BEST PROJECTIONS AT PRESS TIME.

Q ···· What an odd way to experience the war.

A ···· Well, exactly. When I got back from my tour of the war zone, my wife asked me how I'd felt. I told her I'd felt like Brooke Shields — and proudly unrolled the commendations I'd received.

Then it suddenly dawned on me that for the first time in my life, I had attracted institutional approval, and worse, that that approval had come from my first target all those years ago — the military establishment. Frankly, I can do without that kind of cheap irony in my life.

"To Garry Trudeau, for significant contributions to the morale of the United States forces deployed on Operation Desert Storm....We are proud to induct you into our ranks as an honorary BANDIT for life."

—*Certificate of Achievement
4th Battalion 67th Armor
Kuwait City*

A war zone keepsake from Elvis's old unit.

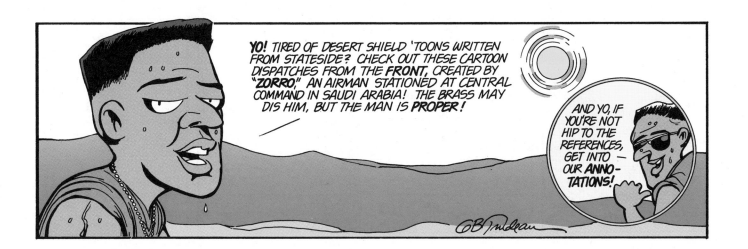

Iranian graphics were no match for Centcom's.

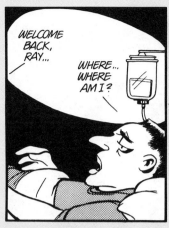

Mission accomplished: 1991's most critically acclaimed piece of cake.

267

Club Scud:
Home of the
$100
hamburger.

OKAY, WE'RE NOW LOOKING AT SOME COCKPIT FOOTAGE FROM AN OPTICALLY GUIDED MISSILE LAUNCHED FROM AN F-117A STEALTH FIGHTER...

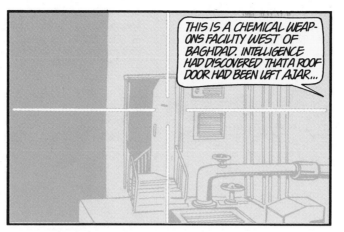

THIS IS A CHEMICAL WEAPONS FACILITY WEST OF BAGHDAD. INTELLIGENCE HAD DISCOVERED THAT A ROOF DOOR HAD BEEN LEFT AJAR...

AS YOU CAN SEE, THE MISSILE ACCESSES THE FACILITY, THREADS ITS WAY DOWN A STAIRWELL, THEN BACK UP A NARROW HEATING DUCT...

...PAST STARTLED IRAQI PRODUCTION MANAGERS AND INTO THE OFFICE OF THE FACILITY ADMINISTRATOR.

UNFORTUNATELY, IT CONTINUES THROUGH AN OPEN WINDOW AND EXPLODES IN A NEARBY PARKING LOT.

STILL, YA GOTTA BE IMPRESSED...

GENERAL, ARE WE WINNING THE WAR?

OPERATION
DESERT STORM
DOD JIB/CENTCOM PAO
MEDIA

Roland B. Hedley, Jr.
NAME
GDS None
SPONSOR NEXT OF KIN
O 734-M-21743
BLOOD TYPE PHR. NO.
Maj E. "Buzz" Fogg
CHAPERONE

LIMITED ACCESS
MUST BE ACCOMPANIED BY PAO OFFICER
WARNING: UNILATERALS WILL BE DE-ACCREDITED

Beating CNN with the latest S-2 IPB's and TLAM-C BDA's. Unilaterals got benched.

Don't shoot, I'm yours.
B.D. had a rocky re-entry.

THAT'S RIGHT, 'RENTS! IT'S THE RETURN OF YOUR LONG-LOST ZONKSTER!

DEAR... WHAT ARE YOU DOING HERE?

MOVING BACK HOME, MOM O' MINE! THE REAL WORLD DIDN'T WORK OUT. BUT HEY, IT HAPPENS!

BOY, I MISSED YOU GUYS BIG TIME! AND THE OL' HOMESTEAD. HERE, MOM, I BROUGHT THIS FOR YOU!

UM... THANK YOU, DEAR. WHAT...

NO STARCH, PLEASE. BOY, I'M STARVED!

SO I SAID TO MIKE, "HEY, I DON'T NEED THIS! AT HOME, THE RENT'S FREE, MOM DOES THE LAUNDRY, AND I CAN EAT ALL I WANT!"

THE TRUTH IS, FOLKS, I HADN'T APPRECIATED WHAT A GREAT DEAL HOME IS! BELIEVE ME, I WON'T EVER MAKE THAT MISTAKE AGAIN!

I LOVE HIM, BUT CAN WE GET A COURT ORDER?

I'LL CALL THE LAWYER. YOU CUT OFF HIS FOOD SUPPLY.

SON, BEFORE YOU UNPACK, LET'S TALK ABOUT THIS...

ABOUT WHAT, POP?

WHAT HAPPENED TO YOU? WHY HAVE YOU COME HOME?

I LOST MY JOB, POP. MIKE COULDN'T AFFORD TO KEEP A BABY SITTER ANYMORE.

WAIT A MINUTE. YOU WERE BABY-SITTING IN NEW YORK?

RIGHT.

YOU SAID YOU HAD YOUR OWN HIT TV SERIES.

I DIDN'T WANT YOU GUYS TO WORRY!

A LOT OF PEOPLE SAID IT COULDN'T BE DONE!

THEY SAID **NOBODY** PUTS AIR BAGS IN MINIVANS! IT'S **TOO TOUGH** TO ENGINEER!

CHRYSLER SAYS, SO **WHAT** IF EVERYBODY ELSE WANTS TO WAIT!

SOME THINGS YA WAIT FOR! PASSENGER-SIDE AIR BAGS IN MINIVANS? OKAY, YA WAIT FOR THOSE. DRIVER-SIDE AIR BAGS? **YA DON'T WAIT!**

BUT, CHAIRMAN IACOCCA — **YOU** WAITED FOR 18 YEARS! **NOBODY** IN THE INDUSTRY FOUGHT AIR BAGS HARDER! AND YOU **LED** THE CHARGE AGAINST STRUCTURAL SAFETY STANDARDS FOR MINIVANS! WHAT **GIVES** HERE?

CUT!

WHAT? WHAT? WOULDN'T A BOARD MEMBER TAKE HIM ON?

ACTORS!

66 *I see Doonesbury is going to do a column on why did I wait 18 years when I had the technology in my pocket. Well, that's bullshit.* 99

—LEE IACOCCA
Chrysler Chairman

273

November 13 **1991**

Scores of newspapers and commentators denounce a *Doonesbury* series on the treatment of Brett Kimberlin, a Federal prisoner who had made accusations about Dan Quayle and possible drug use. "The truth or falsity of Mr. Kimberlin's drug charges is not the issue," opined *The New York Times*. "What's in question is the credibility of the Justice Department's explanation for his severe discipline."

> **"** *It is well known that Garry Trudeau has a personal vendetta against me.* **"**

— DAN QUAYLE

275

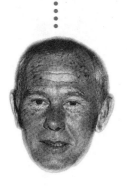

THAT'S RIGHT, CAMPERS. IF YOU'VE EVER SLEPT WITH A PRESIDENTIAL HOPEFUL — OR KNOW SOMEONE *ELSE* WHO HAS — WE WANT TO GIVE YOU $25 IN *COLD, HARD CASH!*

TO FIND OUT IF YOUR STORY IS PRURIENT ENOUGH TO QUALIFY, JUST FILL OUT THE ATTACHED "*TRASH-FOR-CASH*" ENTRY FORM AND SEND IT TO ME, CARE OF THIS PAPER! *GOOD LUCK!*

CAMPAIGN '92 — TRASH FOR CASH

1. **I have trash on:** (CHECK ONE)
   - ☐ Bill Clinton
   - ☐ Paul Tsongas
   - ☐ Jerry Brown
   - ☐ Tom Harkin
   - ☐ Bob Kerrey
   - ☐ George Bush

2. **My story involves:**
   - ☐ me
   - ☐ my best friend
   - ☐ my evil twin
   - ☐ my publicist
   - ☐ a Republican operative
   - ☐ Geraldo

3. **I would describe my relationship with the candidate as:**
   - ☐ torrid, steamy
   - ☐ a defining moment
   - ☐ the right thing to do
   - ☐ videotaped
   - ☐ in litigation

4. **The candidate used to call me:**
   - ☐ "Babe"
   - ☐ "Mommy"
   - ☐ "Commissioner"
   - ☐ from convenience store pay phones

TO BE CONTINUED.

OKAY, BOYS AND GIRLS, HERE'S PART TWO OF OUR CAMPAIGN '92 "*TRASH-FOR-CASH*" ENTRY BLANK! FILL IT IN AND SEND IT TO ME, CARE OF THIS PAPER! IF WE USE YOUR STORY, WE'LL SEND YOU 25 *BIG ONES!*

CAMPAIGN '92 — TRASH FOR CASH

5. **My relationship with the candidate lasted:**
   - ☐ 12 years
   - ☐ 60 days
   - ☐ 60 seconds
   - ☐ Not sure

6. **The last thing that the candidate said to me was:**
   - ☐ "This will not stand."
   - ☐ "Need a job?"
   - ☐ "Cuomo's acting like an Italian-American stereotype."
   - ☐ "Message: I care."
   - ☐ "What's that whirring sound?"

7. **I believe my story will:**
   - ☐ restore my good name
   - ☐ help me find a husband
   - ☐ make my parents proud
   - ☐ get me a record deal
   - ☐ benefit mankind

8. **My name is:**
   - ☐ Gennifer with a "G"
   - ☐ Jennifer with a "J"
   - ☐ Kandy with a "K"
   - ☐ Carrii with two "i's"
   - ☐ Karee with a "K", one "r" and two "e's"
   - ☐ Other _____

CLIP 'N' SEND *TODAY!* ACT NOW, AND YOU'LL BE ELIGIBLE FOR A *FREE SCREEN TEST!*

OKAY, NOW FOR THE TOUGH PART, GANG — THE ESSAY QUESTIONS! PLEASE READ SILENTLY WHILE I READ ALOUD...

CAMPAIGN '92 — TRASH FOR CASH

9. You're dating a married father of three with presidential ambitions. You believe that you and he have a future together. Explain.

10. Name three movies *besides* "Pretty Woman" that have helped shape your personal philosophy.

YOU MAY NOW *BEGIN!* REMINDER TO ALL YOU GENNIFERS: SPELLING COUNTS!

HOW DOES $25 SOUND?

June 1992

J. Edgar Williams, of Chatham County, NC, files a complaint with the Federal Election Commission against Trudeau, Trudeau's syndicate, and every newspaper carrying *Doonesbury*, contending that two strips carrying Jerry Brown's 1-800 number amounted to millions of dollars in free advertising and violated campaign finance laws. The two strips did keep Brown volunteers busy answering phones. "It was great," said Brown press secretary Ileana Wachtel. "It brought in a lot of contributions."

February 1992

When a *Doonesbury* strip encourages readers to seek Texas residency, over 45,000 Texan wannabes send in coupons from all 50 states, Canada, Brazil, Japan, and Kuwait. Texas Controller John Sharp refuses to give the names of Pennsylvania applicants to tax officials from that state, who want "to see if they had paid their state income taxes."

Mr. John Sharp
State Comptroller
Box 13528, Capitol Station
Austin, Texas 78711

Dear Mr. Sharp:
Howdy! I'd like to become a Texan. I hereby solemnly swear that it is my intention to live in Texas at some later date. (I understand there is no legal requirement that I actually do so, and can change my mind later without tax penalty.) Please send me a certificate of residency without delay.
Sincerely,

NAME

MAILING ADDRESS *(BUT NOT WHERE MY HEART IS.)*

CITY   STATE   ZIP

American Cancer Society takes on Mr. Butts as spokesproduct for the Great American Smokeout.

Just say yes: Prevention through irony.

YOU SEE, MY FRIEND, PEOPLE *EXPECT* ACTION FROM ROSS PEROT! THAT'S WHAT MY LIFE'S BEEN ALL ABOUT! LET ME GIVE YOU AN EXAMPLE...

IN 1978, TWO OF MY EMPLOYEES WERE JAILED IN IRAN. SO I HIRED A PARAMILITARY TEAM TO GO IN THERE, FOMENT A JAILHOUSE RIOT, AND GET OUR PEOPLE SAFELY OUT.

THE OPERATION WAS A *BIG* SUCCESS! AND YOU KNOW WHAT LESSON I DREW FROM THAT EXPERIENCE?

BUSINESSMEN SHOULD HAVE THEIR OWN ARMIES?

CORRECT. I'D OFFER TAX CREDITS TO CEO'S.

MR. PEROT, COULD YOU BE A LITTLE MORE SPECIFIC ABOUT HOW YOU WOULD PROPOSE TO WIN THE NATION'S DRUG WAR?

NO. SPECIFICS ARE FOR SMALL MINDS. AMERICA'S OWNERS WANT *BOLD* ACTION, NOT ANOTHER THUMB-SUCKING WHITE PAPER.

THE OWNERS OF THIS COUNTRY ARE GOING TO TAKE BACK THEIR STREETS, AND BELIEVE ME, IT *WON'T* BE PRETTY!

SOUNDS OMINOUS. ANY IMPLICATIONS FOR THE BILL OF RIGHTS?

THE WHAT?

THE OWNER'S MANUAL.

YES?

HI, I'M YOUR PAPER BOY, SIR. I'M HERE TO FIX THE DISHWASHER!

YES?

AVON CALLING! I'M HERE TO RENOVATE YOUR DEN.

YES?

FIRE DEPARTMENT, MA'AM. I'M HERE TO TUNE YOUR LAWNMOWER.

YES?

HI, I'M A SOFTWARE SALESMAN! I'M HERE TO FIX THE GOVERNMENT!

GOOD GOD... WHO'S *THAT?*

OH, NO... IT'S THE COMMISSIONER OF COMICS!

WHAT'S *SHE* WANT?

CHECKING US FOR FAMILY VALUES, NO DOUBT. I'LL BET WE'RE ABOUT TO LOSE OUR ACCREDITATION.

THIS IS *SO* UNFAIR! OUR FAMILY IS INTACT, NORMAL...

YEAH, WELL, APPARENTLY SHE DOESN'T KNOW THAT.

QUICK! GO GET WHAT'S-HER-FACE!

ALEX. YOUR DAUGHTER'S NAME IS ALEX.

NOW YOU'VE DONE IT!

ME? WHO MOUTHED OFF ABOUT BEING PRO-CHOICE

IF YOU ASK ME, THIS WHOLE THING IS

YEAH, WELL, THAT'S JUST THE KIND OF LANGUAGE THAT

WHAT IS THIS— THE N.E.A? I

THIS IS A FAMILY

WHAT WILL WE

BEATS ME. TOO OLD GOLF. NUTS!

THIS FEATURE CONDEMNED BY ORDER OF THE COMMISSIONER OF COMICS

HI, HONEY!

HI, DREAM-BOAT! WHAT'S HAPPENING?

MY MARRIAGE, FOR ONE THING!

HEE, HEE! WHAT DO YOU WANT TO DO TODAY?

I DUNNO— WHAT DO *YOU* WANT TO DO?

I'VE GOT AN IDEA! LET'S GO DOWNTOWN AND HURL EPITHETS AT PEOPLE DIFFERENT FROM US!

WE HAVE A NEW WRITER, I TAKE IT.

HEY, AT LEAST WE'RE BACK.

Diego Tutweiller

WAITE A MINUT!
WAITE A MINUT!

MR. PRESIDENT, WOULD YOU LIKE TO ATTACK GOVERNOR CLINTON AGAIN, OR SHALL WE GO TO OUR CALLERS?

LET'S GO TO THE CALLERS, LARRY...

...AND I'LL TELL YOU WHY. THE CALLERS ARE GOOD, DECENT AMERICANS. NOT SAYING THIS BIG-SPENDING DEMOCRAT GUY ISN'T. WOULDN'T DO THAT. NOT PRUDENT.

EVEN THOUGH, GOTTA SAY, TRIPS TO MOSCOW, MEETINGS, RAISES QUESTIONS. BUT, HEY, DON'T CRY FOR ME, LEONID. WAS THERE AN UNPATRIOTIC ANGLE? CAN'T SAY. WOULDN'T BE FAIR.

©B Trudeau

UM... OKAY. OUR FIRST CALLER IS...

KGB? TREASON? CAN'T SAY. DON'T HAVE THE FACTS.

I'M NOT DOING THIS FOR MYSELF. THE PRESIDENCY IS A THANKLESS, DIRTY JOB, BUT I'M WILLING TO MAKE A WORLD-CLASS SACRIFICE IF THE PEOPLE BEG ME...

CLIK!

OUR ENTIRE PRIME-TIME SCHEDULE TONIGHT IS BEING PRE-EMPTED BY PART THREE OF "THE PEOPLE'S SERVANT"...

IT'S JUST THAT SIMPLE!

CLIK!

WORLD PEACE? STRICTLY ROUTINE. NO BIG DEAL.

JUST OPEN UP THE HOOD AND FIX IT! END OF STORY!

CLIK! CLIK!

©B Trudeau

WELCOME TO THE 24-HOUR PEROT CHANNEL!

YOU'RE GONNA HEAR A GIANT SUCKING SOUND, SEE?

E.D. 003 C.D. 08

CHUNKA!

CLINTON!

CHUNKA!

BUSH!

FLUSH!

FLUSH?

PEROT!

©B Trudeau

December **1992**

Working Woman magazine names *Doonesbury's* Joanie Caucus and Lacey Davenport as among the best role models for women.

> "I want to be myself, and it doesn't help to have something like *Doonesbury* start the morning. I'm sure God is at this point very angry with Garry Trudeau."

— ATTORNEY GENERAL
JANET RENO

HEY, **KIDS**! EVER AMAZED BY SOME OF THE PRODUCTION VALUES IN THIS FEATURE? EVER WONDER HOW IT'S ALL DONE?

FOR INSTANCE, TAKE OUR WHITE HOUSE TABLEAU. LOOKS LIKE A COSTLY LOCATION SET-UP, RIGHT?

LOOK AGAIN! IT'S NOTHING BUT A TINY SCALE MODEL OF THE REAL THING!

THE MAGIC OF MINIATURES — A KEY ELEMENT OF BIG-TIME CARTOONING!

WELCOME TO THE WHITE HOUSE!

HEE, HEE! THAT'S "BILL CLINTON" SPEAKING! BY PUTTING WORDS IN HIS MOUTH, WE CAN OFFER TIMELY POLITICAL SATIRE!

I CAN FEEL YOUR PAIN!

OF COURSE, WHAT **REALLY** COUNTS ARE THE REGULAR CHARACTERS...

AIEE!

GB Trudeau

Foamboard and mirrors:
Deconstructing the magic.

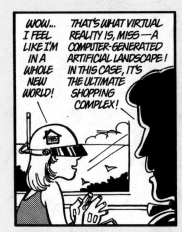

WE JUST GOT ANOTHER PICTURE OF ALEX FROM J.J.—IT'S PRETTY CUTE...

HOW'S EVERYONE DOING?

WELL, NOT SO GREAT, ACTUALLY. MIKE STILL HASN'T FOUND A PERMANENT JOB.

I'M A LITTLE WORRIED ABOUT HIM. BEING OUT OF WORK THAT LONG CAN GRIND YOU DOWN. IT CAN CHANGE YOU.

HONEY? I'M GOING OUT TO DO THE SHOP-LIFTING!

WE NEED MILK.

THE FACE OF UNEMPLOYMENT 1992
IT AIN'T PRETTY

Post-rock bottom:
Downsizing in the '90s.

OH, MIKE... YOU'RE NOT ACTUALLY DOING SUPERMARKET PULL-OUTS NOW, ARE YOU?

HEY, WHAT'S WRONG WITH THAT? I'M PROUD OF THEM! SOME OF THESE SMALL JOBS ARE AMONG THE BEST WORK I'VE DONE!

IT'S TRUE, MOM! DAD JUST DID A REALLY NEAT AD FOR A CHILDREN'S THEATER!

I DID?

HE DID?

"LIVE SHOWS HOURLY— GIRLS! GIRLS! GIRLS!"

UM...RIGHT! AND THOSE LADIES ARE THEIR MOM-MIES!

ON THEIR WAY TO THE BEACH.

MOM, IT'S JUST GETTING WORSE. IT'S LIKE MIKE HAS PUT HIS INTEGRITY IN A LITTLE BOX AND STORED IT AWAY...

NOW, DEAR, MIKE'S JUST TRYING TO SUPPORT HIS FAMILY...

I KNOW, BUT IT'S LIKE HE'LL TAKE ANY JOB NOW — NO MATTER **WHO** THE CLIENT!

NOW, NOW, THAT DOESN'T SOUND LIKE MIKE?...

WHO'S THAT ON THE PHONE?

SOME TERRORIST GROUP. THEY NEED A LEAF-LET DONE.

BY WHEN?

293

August 1993

A Santa Barbara skateboard shop gets in trouble with a customer's mother for selling a pirated "Mr. Butts" skateboard. Owner of the shop Michael Magne defends himself: "It's not that big a deal. It's a joke. There's no other way to take it unless you're a moron." He urges a reporter, "Make us look like we're straight from hell because that's the best kind of press. The kids are going to look at us like Gods."

A SUMMER FANTASY...

$10 MILLION? WOW... THANKS, MYSTERY WO-MAN!

PLEASE, CALL ME CONTESSA.

AN INNOCENT INVITATION...

COULD I BUY YOU AN ESPRESSO, CONTESSA? IN SEATTLE, SAY?

A DECENT CUP OF COFFEE...

$10 MILLION! WHAT AM I GO-ING TO DO WITH $10 MILLION?

AN INDECENT PROPOSAL.

WHAT THE HEY— I'VE STILL GOT $9 MILLION LEFT!

THE CONTESSA HAS A CHANGE OF HEART...

WHAT I DID WAS FOR LOVE, MIKE. I CANNOT ACCEPT YOUR MONEY. INVEST IN AMERICA.

OKAY.

AND SO HE DID.

HEY, MAN, HAVE YOU **REALLY** PUT HUNDREDS OF INNER CITY KIDS THROUGH MED SCHOOL?

NO BIG DEAL.

NO BIG DEAL? MAN, YOU'RE SPENDIN' YOUR LIFE HELPIN' HOMIES OUTA THE HOOD, WHEN YOU COULD BE SIT-TIN' IN A POOL UP IN SANTA BARBARA!

GOOD POINT.

CLOSURE.

SO HOW'VE YOU BEEN, CONTESSA?

GRAVELY ILL. MY LIFE WAS SAVED BY A BRILLIANT, YOUNG BLACK SURGEON.

MIKE'S SUMMER FANTASY HAS HIM POWER-BREAKFASTING AT L.A.'S FOUR SEASONS HOTEL.

... AND I SEE MICHAEL DOUGLAS PLAYING ME!

SUDDENLY...

HI.

GOOD LORD! IT'S ... IT'S **SHARON STONE!**

I SAW YOU ACROSS THE ROOM. I WANT YOU. NOW.

NOW?

CALL FOR YOU, MR. DOONES-BURY!

MIKE? BILL CLINTON! YOUR COUNTRY NEEDS YOU! NOW!

UH... NOW?

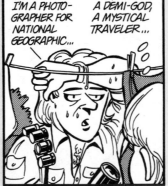

Panel 1:
TIME TO PAY THE BILLS, FRANCESCA. THE LIGHT IS ALMOST PERFECT BEHIND THAT WASHED-OUT COVERED BRIDGE...

GOD, WHAT *IS* IT ABOUT YOU, ROBERT KINCAID?

Panel 2:
OUT HERE IN THE NATURAL WORLD, IT'S JUST THE "SHOOTER" AGAINST CHANGING LIGHT CONDITIONS...

THE POWER, THE RAW ENERGY, THE THIGHS!

Panel 3:
BY USING PROFESSIONAL FILTERS AND LENSES, I TRY TO DOMINATE THE SCENE, BEND IT TO MY DESIRES. HERE COMES THE LIGHT... STEADY... STEADY...

WOW... LOOK AT HIM SHAPE THE IMAGE TO HIS VISION...

Panel 4:
GOT IT! IT'S *MINE!* I *OWN* IT!

OWN ME! OWN *ME!*

CLIK! CLIK! CLIK! CLIK!

Panel 5:
YOU SEE, YOU CAN'T JUST *TAKE* PHOTOS, FRANCESCA. YOU MUST *OWN* THEM, IMPOSE YOUR WILL ON THE SCENE!

LOOK AT THE LIGHT CATCH THE TINY HAIRS ON HIS FOREARMS...

Panel 6:
LIKE I DID IN HUE, IN BEIRUT, IN THE AMAZON BASIN, ON THE STEPPES OF THE UKRAINE, IN THE RUINS OF OUTER DZEHZKAZGAN!

YOU'RE LIKE SOME STAR CREATURE, ROBERT KINCAID, SOME SHAMAN!

Panel 7:
I'M ONE OF THE LAST COWBOYS. ONE DAY, COMPUTERS AND ROBOTS WILL RUN EVERYTHING. RACHEL CARSON WAS RIGHT. SO WERE JOHN MUIR AND ALDO LEOPOLD!

HIS OPINIONS, SO DEEP, SO VIRILE...

Panel 8:
DID I MENTION I LOVE FRESH VEGETABLES—AND W.B. YEATS?

I AM NOT WORTHY, I AM NOT WORTHY...

Panel 9:
FRANCESCA, COME AWAY WITH ME! COME WITH ME TO BATDAMBANG, RAWALPINDI, ZAGROS AND ADDIS ABABA!

I CAN'T, ROBERT KINCAID, I HAVE RESPONSIBILITIES.

Panel 10:
BESIDES, YOU ARE THE HIGHWAY, THE ROAD. GOING WITH YOU WOULD KILL THE WILD, MAGNIFICENT ANIMAL THAT IS YOU! GO, ROBERT KINCAID, GO LIKE THE WIND!

Panel 11:
IF THAT'S WHAT YOU WANT, I'LL BE SENSITIVE TO YOUR NEEDS. I'LL ALWAYS LOVE YOU, FRANCESCA!

AND I YOU, ROBERT KINCAID.

Panel 12:
I'LL NEVER FORGET THE WAY YOU FILLED OUT YOUR JEANS!

AND I'LL RECALL YOUR OPEN SHIRT, THIGHS AND FOREARMS! NOW, *GO!*

CLIK!

YOU COULD GET A FRESH START! RE-TRAIN!

*A one o'clock with Bdippl
at Cafe Fwiblob.*

299

For Mark, a shiny, brand-new
sexual orientation.

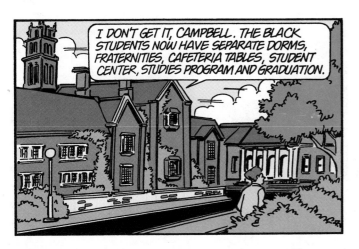

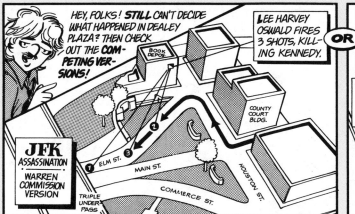

BOOPSIE IS READING FOR "TONYA: MY WAY."

"I'M SOMEBODY: I'M A PERSON WITH A / DREAM!"

"NOBODY EVER GAVE ME ANYTHING. I HAD TO WORK HARD FOR 20 YEARS TO GET WHERE I AM TODAY. NOBODY CAN TAKE THAT AWAY FROM ME, NOBODY!"

OKAY, GOOD, GOOD... NOW SKIP DOWN TO THE BOTTOM OF THE PAGE AND READ THAT LAST SPEECH...

"YOU HEARD ME—WHACK THE LITTLE TWIT!"

MAKE A NOTE, IF SHE'S INNOCENT, JEFF GETS THAT LINE.

OKAY, BABE, IN THIS NEXT SCENE, YOU'RE FLASHING BACK EIGHT YEARS...

YOU'RE PRACTICING AT FOUR IN THE MORNING. LIFE IS TOUGH, NOBODY BELIEVES IN YOU, BUT THE DREAM WON'T DIE, GOT IT?

I THINK SO.

BY THE WAY, THESE SCENES ARE PLAYED IN THE NUDE.

TONYA SKATED IN THE NUDE?

HAD TO. SHE COULDN'T AFFORD THE COSTUMES.

OKAY, MS. BOOPSTEIN, LET'S HAVE YOU READ JUST ONE MORE SPEECH—TONYA'S FAREWELL AT LILLEHAMMER. FROM THE TOP OF PAGE 117, PLEASE!

"SKATING IN THE OLYMPICS WAS ALWAYS MY DREAM. IT WAS THE DREAM THAT KEPT ME GOING. SKATING HERE WAS THAT DREAM'S FULFILLMENT..."

"THE DREAM OF GOING TO THE OLYMPICS IS OVER! IT IS A DREAM COME TRUE! NOW I HAVE A DIFFERENT DREAM, A SHINY, **NEW** DREAM..."

"I DREAM OF... OF... NOT GOING TO JAIL!"

BIGGER! SHE'S **PUMPED!**

GOOD MORNING. LIKE MUCH OF THE MEDIA, THIS FEATURE HAS LONG BEEN FASCINATED BY THE TORTUOUS CAREER OF *RICHARD NIXON*...

JOIN US NOW AS WE REVISIT SOME OF OUR FAVORITE EPISODES DEPICTING THE LIFE AND TIMES OF OUR LATE PRESIDENT.

ONE SMALL NOTE: SOME OF THE STRIPS HAVE BEEN SLIGHTLY REVISED TO BRING THEM UP TO CONTEMPORARY STANDARDS...

THAT ASIDE, THEY'RE *EXACTLY* AS THEY ORIGINALLY APPEARED!

FROM MAY 29, 1973...

HE'S ~~GUILTY! GUILTY! GUILTY! GUILTY!~~ FLAWED, FLAWED, FLAWED, FLAWED!

FAVORITE NIXON STRIPS.* FROM MAY 21, 1974...

OF COURSE, DIFFERENT PEOPLE WILL HAVE DIFFERING MEMORIES OF WHAT WAS SAID — ESPECIALLY AT THE SO-CALLED HUSH-MONEY MEETING.

IN THIS MEETING, WE CANDIDLY DISCUSSED THE OPTIONS. FIRST, WE COULD HAVE PAID THE MONEY, IN THE INTERESTS OF NATIONAL SECURITY. BUT WE MIGHT HAVE BEEN BLED DRY...

SECONDLY, WE COULD HAVE TAKEN EVERYONE WITH ANY KNOWLEDGE OF THE CASE OUTSIDE AND SHOT THEM...

...BUT AS A ~~LAWYER~~ HUMANITARIAN I KNEW THAT WOULD BE *WRONG!*

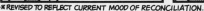
* REVISED TO REFLECT CURRENT MOOD OF RECONCILIATION.

FROM JULY 23, 1974.*

"NO IMPEACHABLE OFFENSE"! HOW CAN HIS LAWYER KEEP *BAB-BLING* THAT?

NIXON LEFT *NO* PART OF THE CONSTITUTION *UN-TRAMPLED!*

OBSTRUCTION OF JUSTICE, HUSH MONEY PAYMENTS, SECRET BOMBINGS, 25 TOP AIDES CONVICTED OR INDICTED...

MY LORD, WHAT DOES IT TAKE? WHAT DOES IT *TAKE?*

≥ SIGH... ≥

~~IF ONLY HE'D KNOCK OVER A BANK OR SOMETHING...~~ *BOY,* HE'S CONTROVERSIAL!

~~BY GEORGE, WE'D HAVE HIM THEN!~~ I'LL SAY!

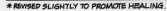
* REVISED SLIGHTLY TO PROMOTE HEALING.

HE'S LYING RIGHT NOW, ISN'T HE?

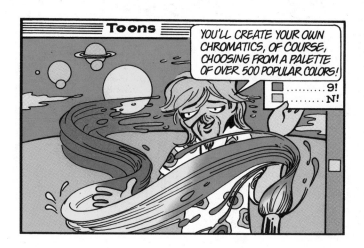

... AND FINALLY, TO PARENTS HERE TODAY, A BIT OF ADVICE: SUFFER YOUR CHILDREN GLADLY.

IF THEY DO NOT MAKE THEIR WAY OUT INTO THE WORLD IMMEDIATELY, IT IS BECAUSE THE WORLD HAS BECOME SUCH A FORBIDDING PLACE IN THESE TIMES...

NEVER HAS A CLASS GRADUATED INTO SUCH AN UNCERTAIN AND BLEAK ECONOMIC ENVIRONMENT...

HOW BLEAK? WELL, THIS YEAR ONLY A SINGLE COMPANY RECRUITED ON CAMPUS, DOWN FROM TWO LAST YEAR!

WE ARE, OF COURSE, DEEPLY GRATEFUL TO THE REMAINING EMPLOYER FOR ITS COMMITMENT TO OUR FINE GRADUATES...

GAP! GAP! GAP! GAP!

WOOF! WOOF! WOOF!

... BUT LOSING McDONALD'S WAS A BLOW.

From Woodstock to Woodstock:
What a long, strange strip it's been.

"What process of disenchantment led to this portrayal of the leader of the free world as a levitating cake?"
—*New York Times editorial, August 23, 1994*

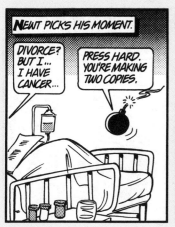

TRY TO UNDERSTAND—THIS WAS ARKANSAS.

Q .... We're running out of book. Whither the comics?

A .... If comics were important to a pre-literate America, they're absolutely indispensible to a post-literate one. When people tell me they keep up with the news through *Doonesbury*, I tremble for the republic, but the truth is, everyone has time for the comics. They get under people's skin. My favorite readers are the sort who write to complain that I've been wrong every day for the last 20 years. That's a long time to chew sandpaper, but you'd be surprised how many people do it.

July 8 **1995**

The University of California releases documents that allegedly claim that tobacco giant Brown & Williamson hid knowledge of the addictive properties of nicotine. The documents had been sent to UC-San Francisco Professor Stanton Glantz. The only return address listed was "Mr. Butts."

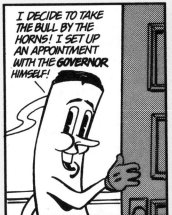

Q .... Lyndon Johnson once said that it was better to have would-be critics inside the tent pissing out than outside pissing in. Where do you stand on co-option?

A .... When I first started drawing President Clinton as a waffle, the AP ran a story about how I had jeopardized my standing with the Adminstration, and that I was unlikely to be asked to any more White House dinners. When a friend of mine expressed surprise that I had *ever* been invited by the Clintons to dinner, I replied that I hadn't — that, in fact, if I had been, this whole nasty business with the waffle could have been avoided.

WHAT YOU HAVE TO RE-MEMBER IS THAT IN THOSE DAYS, HOLLYWOOD HAD FAMILY VALUES COMING OUT THE WAZOO...

THERE WASN'T MUCH RISK-TAKING. IT TOOK A LOT OF GUTS TO GET BEHIND THE KIND OF FILMS WE WANTED TO MAKE. SO WHEN THE KID HIT TOWN, WE TOOK NOTICE!

HERE, FINALLY, WAS SOMEONE WILLING TO PUT HIS MONEY WHERE HIS MOUTH WAS. THE GUY WAS FOR REAL!

SO PHIL GRAMM WAS A PLAYER?

IN THE SEX-SPOOF WORLD? HE *RULED!*

SID, WHY DID PHIL GRAMM GET INTO THE FILM BUSINESS?

WELL, I THINK HE HAD THE BUG...

ALSO, HE JUST LOVED SA-TIRE. HE FIRST GOT INTER-ESTED IN US WHEN HE SAW "TRUCK STOP WOMEN," OUR SPOOF POKING FUN AT INTERSTATE COMMERCE.

WHEN WE FINALLY GOT DOWN TO MAKING "WHITE HOUSE MADNESS," HE CALLED ME UP AND SAID, "IT'S GOT TO BE A SPOOF. I'M COMMITTED TO MAKING SPOOFS!"

SO THE FINAL PRODUCT?

TWO HOURS OF NON-STOP SPOOFING.

THANKS FOR TALK-ING TO US, SID...

NOT AT ALL. WHEN DO YOU AIR?

TONIGHT. YOU DON'T HAVE A COPY OF "WHITE HOUSE MAD-NESS," DO YOU? WE'LL NEED A CLIP...

NO, I LOST MY COPY IN A MUD SLIDE.

KNOW WHERE WE CAN FIND ONE?

HMM...NOT REALLY. YOUR BEST BET IS THE PERSONAL LI-BRARY OF SOME SPOOF COLLECTOR...

WELL, IF YOU THINK OF ANY...

TRY THE CLAR-ENCE THOMAS COLLECTION! HIS CURATOR'S AN OLD PAL OF MINE!

66 *People are going to attack you. It just happens.* **99**

— SEN. PHIL GRAMM
on his treatment in Doonesbury

Senators John McCain and Bob Kerrey rise on the Senate floor to denounce Trudeau for his strip on Bob Dole's campaign strategy to exploit his war record. Says McCain: "Suffice it to say that I hold him in utter contempt."

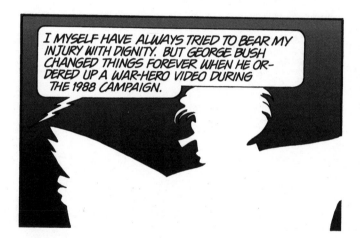

YOU KNOW, IF VOTERS HAVE SENT US ONE MESSAGE LOUD AND CLEAR...

...IT'S THAT THEY'RE TIRED OF GOVERNMENT INSPECTORS TELLING THEM WHAT TO EAT, DRINK AND BREATHE!

TAKE SPOILED MEAT— IT COSTS US 4,000 LIVES, 5 MILLION ILLNESSES AND OVER $3 BILLION IN MEDICAL EXPENSES YEARLY.

BUT DOES THAT JUSTIFY THE HORRIFIC REGULATORY BURDEN ON THE MEAT INDUSTRY? COULDN'T WE LIVE WITH 8,000 DEATHS? OR 12,000?

AMERICANS ARE **CRYING OUT** FOR COST-BENEFIT RATIOS THAT MAKE SENSE TO BUSINESS! IF I'M ELECT-ED, THEY'LL GET 'EM!

BOB DOLE FOR PRESIDENT.

BECAUSE WE ALL HAVE TO DIE OF SOMETHING.

❝ *I think it was in poor taste, but, you know, everybody has to make a living.* **❞**

— BOB DOLE

331

PHOTOGRAPHY CREDITS

Matthew Klein: 11, 19, 33, 47, 58, 77, 78, 82, 83, 100, 101, 107, 123, 135, 159, 171, 183, 187, 212, 244, 256, 258, 261, 264, 267, 268, 270, 283, 289, 293, 299. **FPG:** 27, Carson Baldwin; 84, Oscar Nelder; 96, Newsworld/New York Tribune; 104, Newsworld/New York Tribune; 109, Paul Kern; 113, FPG Int'l; 137, Isaiah Karlinsky; 167, Peter Borsari; 173, Mike Valeri; 175, Laurence Agron; 176, Mark Reinstein; 185, Arthur D'Amario III; 196, The News World; 215, Mark Reinstein; 229, Laurence Agron; 235, Laurence Agron; 273, Joe Crachiola; 275, Chris Mooney; 276, Peter Borsari; 288, Mark Reinstein; 305, Mark Reinstein; 311, Mark Reinstein; 329, Mark Reinstein. **Black Star:** 49, Dennis Brack; 73, Dennis Brack; 117, Dennis Brack; 121, Dennis Brack; 147, Dennis Brack; 222, Bill Foley; 231, Lisa Quinones; 249, Rick Friedman; 280, Rick Friedman; 331, Rick Friedman. **AP/Wide World Photos:** 24, 37, 64, 66, 129, 156, 225, 296, 304. **Vireo:** 209, J.H. Dick (Academy of Natural Sciences). **Courtesy of:** 141, *The Recorder*, Greenfield, MA; 164, John Leonard; 205, George Will; 289, White House model from *Mouse House: 5 Easy-To-Build Homes For Your Computer Mouse* by Jim Becker, Andy Mayer and Doug Mayer, illustrations by Dick Witt and Bob Greisen, Penguin Books, 1995. **With permission:** 22, *Chicago Tribune*; 97, *San Francisco Examiner* photo, John Gorman; 177, *Times-Advocate*, Escondido, Ca.